Past Lives
of the
Rich and Famous

ALSO BY SYLVIA BROWNE

Past Lives of the Rich and Famous

Sylvia Browne
with Lindsay Harrison

HARPER LUXE

An Imprint of HarperCollins*Publishers*

This book is metaphysical and philosophical in nature. Nothing herein is intended to imply an endorsement of the book, author, or publisher by any of the persons mentioned herein, including the deceased celebrities and their families.

HarperCollins books may be purchased for educational, business, or sales promotional use. For information, please e-mail the Special Markets Department at SPsales@harpercollins.com.

FIRST HARPERLUXE EDITION

HarperLuxe™ is a trademark of HarperCollins Publishers

Library of Congress Cataloging-in-Publication Data is available upon request.

ISBN: 978-0-06-220159-1

13 14 ID/RRD 10 9 8 7 6 5 4 3 2 1

To my husband, Michael Ulery,
who at long last is the man of my dreams.

Contents

Past Lives
of the
Rich and Famous

PART ONE

The How and Why of Past Lives

I don't ever want you to take my word for it, or anyone else's, when you're exploring and arriving at the fundamental beliefs that resonate in your soul and, most of all, when those beliefs answer more questions than they raise. I want you to keep an open mind, educate yourself on a variety of philosophies, and pay attention to what makes sense to you.

In other words, as you read these pages, I want you to *think*.

How can a child, from a perfectly "normal," unremarkable family, suddenly begin playing the piano with the skill of a virtuoso and composing music at the age of five?

How and why does a three-year-old child born and raised in Alaska develop what turns into a lifelong, passionate curiosity about the American Civil War?

Why are there specific places on earth that you've yearned to go for as long as you can remember, and languages you've yearned to learn, while other places and languages are of no interest to you at all?

How can you land in a strange city you've never been in before and find that, impossibly, you not only feel at home there, you actually seem to know your way around?

Why are there certain people you meet for the first time and have to fight an urge to say, "Hello again! Where have you been?"

Why were you born with your own unique set of preferences and aversions to things that, by definition, you've never been exposed to in this life?

Why, without warning or logic, do you suddenly develop a mortal fear of something you've never been afraid of before, from flying to water to darkness to choking to heights? For that matter, why were you born with any mortal fears at all?

What would prompt a six-year-old child to thank his mother for breakfast by saying, "You're the best of all twelve moms I've ever had"?

Where would a ten-year-old girl come up with a voice and an affinity for singing opera?

Ask those questions to any number of scientists, theologians, psychologists, and other "experts" on human behavior. They're likely to reply with either a blank stare, some double-talk that makes no sense at all, or that common, meaningless response, "It just happens." Wouldn't "I don't have the first clue" be a lot more honest?

I *do* have the first clue. I have an explanation that answers every one of those questions, and thousands more, and I will never understand why there's such reluctance among so many to embrace and celebrate that explanation, because it confirms the promise God made to all of us at the moment our souls were created—very simply, that we are eternal. It doesn't just mean that we always will be from now on. It means we always *have been*. So, accepting the fact that we've always existed, where have we been since the beginning of time? And what have we been doing to occupy ourselves? Nothing? Lying around on clouds playing harps? Really? I don't believe that for one second, and neither do you.

We've each been living life after life after life, in our Home on the Other Side and here on earth as well, on a perpetual, sacred journey toward our spirit's greatest potential, in joyful service to our Creator. He didn't create a random, imperfect, haphazard universe for us to occupy. He presented us with an infinity of perfection and logic. His creation makes sense. It's cyclical, and it's orderly. To suggest, as many theologians do, that at the end of our one and only lifetime, God assesses our performances and decides whether we should be rewarded or punished is to suggest that God, who adores us unconditionally as His own beloved children, gives us one opportunity to please Him, and if we fail, He throws up His hands and banishes us to an eternity of hell. Does that really make sense to you?

Me neither.

I've actually had any number of people say to me, through all these decades of readings, lectures, salons, and television appearances, "Of course I don't believe in reincarnation. I'm a Christian." To which I say, as a fellow (Gnostic) Christian, "So am I! So, *think*!"

Please don't ever get the idea that my absolute belief in reincarnation is arbitrary, something I decided to embrace because that's just how goofy we psychics are. I was brought up in Catholic school. I minored in theology and world religion in college. I've spent my life passionately devouring every religious and spiritual book I can get my hands on, from the teachings of Buddha and Muhammad, to the Tantras, to the Egyptian *Book of the Dead,* to the Talmud and the Koran, to the Bhagavad Gita, to Elaine Pagels's *The Gnostic Gospels,* to the life of Apollonius of Tyana, a Greek spiritual healer and teacher who was a contemporary of Christ. I've studied with priests, yogis, ministers, rabbis, nuns, Tibetan monks, and Zen masters. And I can honestly tell you that as a result of all that and much, much more, my belief in past lives has grown stronger, to the point where I no longer think of it as something I believe; I think of it as something I *know.*

I was especially intrigued to discover that most of the world's great religions—including Christianity, until Pope Constantine restructured it in the sixth century— embrace the truth of reincarnation. It inspired me to return to the Bible and look for the references to reincarnation that I was sure had to be there. I refused to believe that Pope Constantine, no matter how determined he might have been, managed to get his hands on every copy of every translation of the Holy Scripture and toss out everything he didn't agree with.

This search, this insatiable show-me curiosity common to us Missouri natives, led to my becoming a tireless, rabid student of the Bible, all twenty-six versions of it. And as thorough as I'm sure Pope Constantine tried to be, I was delighted to discover that, even in translations of the Bible written after his death, several references to reincarnation remained intact, if you spend a few extra moments looking at them more closely than just giving them a passing glance.

The ninth chapter of John, for example, tells the story of Jesus and his disciples happening upon a man who was born blind. The disciples asked Jesus, "Master, who did sin, this man, or his parents, that he was born blind?"

The disciples, in other words, were curious about the possibility that the man's blindness was a punishment for sins he'd committed. But since he had been blind since birth, what possible opportunity would he have had to commit sins if it weren't in a past life, unless he'd been creative enough to find a way to sin in the womb?

In Matthew 17:11–13 there's an even more obvious reference to reincarnation, during a talk Jesus has with three of his disciples, Peter, James, and John: "'Elijah is indeed coming and will restore all things; but I tell you that Elijah has already come, and they did not recognize him, but they did to him whatever they pleased.' Then the disciples understood that he was speaking to them about John the Baptist."

Now, if Elijah was still coming but had already come, obviously Jesus was referring to two separate incarnations. And "they did not recognize him" as Elijah in that previous incarnation, but "the disciples understood" that Elijah's previous incarnation was a lifetime as John the Baptist, who was imprisoned and beheaded by Herod, the king of Judea. I can't think of a clearer example of "they did to him whatever they pleased" than imprisoning and beheading someone. But more to the point, if Jesus Christ himself accepted reincarnation as the truth, as he clearly did, who are any of us to doubt him? Which brings us back to my original question: Why is there such a common perception that you can be a Christian or you can believe in reincarnation, but you can't do both?

I don't think I ever doubted that we live several lifetimes on earth; I just didn't understand, when I was very young and just starting to wonder about this kind of thing, what difference it would make whether or not I'd lived before, especially if I didn't remember. If I were a geisha in Japan in the 1800s, or the person who invented shoelaces, or the maid of honor at Queen Victoria's wedding, beyond having something new to talk about at cocktail parties, or unless that information is of some use to me in my life today, who cares? Like many people, I read a book about an actual past-life case, entitled *The Search for Bridey Murphy*, and found it fascinating. But again, even if it were true, so what?

For those of you who are too young to remember, in 1952 a woman named Virginia Tighe, in Pueblo, Colorado, volunteered one night at a dinner party to be part of a casual demonstration by a hypnotist named Morey Bernstein. To the shock of Bernstein and all the other guests, the minute she went "under," Virginia Tighe began speaking in a thick brogue and identifying herself as Bridey Murphy, a nineteenth-century woman from Ireland. Throughout the course of subsequent recorded hypnosis sessions in Morey Bernstein's office, Tighe, in the persona of Bridey Murphy, sang Irish songs, told Irish stories, and related intricate details of her life in Cork a hundred years earlier with no prompting or coaching from Bernstein whatsoever. The recordings were eventually translated into more than a dozen languages, and *The Search for Bridey Murphy* hit bestseller lists around the world.

Of course there were efforts to discredit the claims of Morey Bernstein and Virginia Tighe, but they were never very successful. Bernstein, rather than being a notorious fraud, was actually a highly respected businessman who'd been practicing amateur hypnosis for years, purely as a hobby, and was clearly as shocked as everyone else at this new identity his hobby had seemingly unearthed. Virginia Tighe was a twenty-seven-year-old mother of two when the Bridey Murphy sessions began and, rather than leaping at the opportunity to use up every second of her fifteen minutes of fame, she insisted that her real name not be used in

Bernstein's book and rejected countless opportunities to get rich from the phenomenon she'd inadvertently helped create.

It was an enthralling story, and I was as fascinated as everyone else. By then I was a master hypnotist with a thriving hypnosis practice, helping clients with everything from weight loss to quitting smoking, so the hypnotism aspect was frankly more interesting to me than the past life the Bridey Murphy sessions seemed to have accessed.

Many of you are already familiar with where this discussion is headed. I'm not about to presume that everyone who is reading this book is familiar with my previous work so, those of you who aren't newcomers, please forgive the repetition. But it's impossible to discuss past lives in depth without sharing the firsthand experiences that proved to me beyond all doubt—at a point, I should add, when I wasn't even looking for proof or thinking about past lives at all—that reincarnation is a very real, very logical part of our eternity.

A bright, personable accountant came to see me one day for a hypnosis session about a weight problem that had plagued him throughout his adulthood. He went under easily, and I was preparing to give him a number of posthypnotic suggestions that had always proved successful with comfort eaters, as I knew he was, when he began casually telling me in the present tense about his work building pyramids in Egypt. Then, without warning, he lapsed into a stream of nonsense syllables that sounded a lot like Martian to me, and I jumped to the same conclusion you would have: I decided that he must be having a psychotic breakdown of some kind, which was far beyond my areas of expertise. When I eased him out of his hypnotic trance and said goodbye, he seemed perfectly normal again, with no memory of what had happened.

Believing with all my heart that this man needed more help than I could give him, I sent a tape of the session to a friend of mine, a psychology professor at Stanford, for his objective evaluation. When my friend called three days later, I was fully expecting him to suggest rushing my client in for psychiatric help as soon as possible. Instead, to my complete shock, he told me he'd played the tape for three of his colleagues who specialized in linguistics. Working separately and without comparing notes, they'd identified those "nonsense syllables" as a fluent, well-spoken monologue in an ancient Assyrian dialect that would have been common among pyramid builders in ancient Egypt.

If any one experience inspired me to learn the art of hypnotic past-life regressions, it was that accountant pyramid builder. By then I'd established the Nirvana Foundation for Psychic Research, the primary purposes of which were to teach psychic development and to explore and prove the survival of the spirit after death. And what more effective way to establish and underscore the fact that the spirit survives deaths than to confirm the existence of past lives?

I worked and studied regressive hypnosis with an excited passion, and soon I was almost overwhelmed with clients eager to explore their past lives as part of the psychic readings they'd booked. I didn't consider any of these past lives valid until my staff and I had confirmed them through extensive research. If someone claimed to have been a Montana rancher named Clifford Underwood in 1895, for example, we weren't satisfied until we'd established that a Clifford Underwood really did own a ranch in Montana in 1895. Mind you, this was long before computers and Google were at anyone's disposal, so our research involved a whole lot of hours at a whole lot of libraries, public records facilities, and the invaluable San Bruno National Archives. But sooner or later we were able to establish, about 95 percent of the time, that the past lives my clients had revisited had actually occurred. That was, in a way, discovery number one. Discovery number two turned out to be that I'd only begun to scratch the surface of the potential impact of past lives on the clients who experienced them through regressive hypnosis.

A man named Jason came to my office for a reading about a possible career change. He was walking stiffly and wearing a brace to ease the chronic neck pain and spasms he'd been suffering since his early thirties, the cause of which was still a mystery to a parade of doctors to whom he'd paid many thousands of dollars. With his permission I hypnotized him, partly for his relaxation and pain relief but also to add yet another name to my growing list of confirmed past-life regressions, which intrigued him very much when I offered the invitation.

Before long, he was giving me a detailed description of his life as a soldier, blue uniform and all, in the French Revolution in the 1790s. He was a young widower with no children and nothing to lose, which made him a notoriously fearless zealot. After several bloody but victorious battles, he was finally captured and executed at the guillotine when he was thirty-three. Jason was especially moved by his discovery that the wife he'd loved and lost in that life had been the same woman to whom he was happily married in this life, which explained why they'd known from the moment they'd met that they were meant to be together.

A few weeks later I walked offstage from a lecture to find Jason waiting to say hello. He looked wonderful, healthy, and smiling, with his neck brace nowhere in sight. The day after our session, he was eager to tell me, he'd noticed his pain beginning to diminish, and by the fourth day he felt so completely healed that he and his wife had ceremonially burned his neck brace in their fireplace.

I didn't catch on. It took my Spirit Guide, Francine, to piece it together for me. Chronic neck pain, starting in Jason's early thirties. Doctor after doctor unable to find its source, let alone heal it. A previous life that ended at the guillotine when he was thirty-three. Once those facts had been unearthed in Jason's subconscious, where the spirit mind lives, and brought out into the light of day, where they could be explored and dealt with, the pain had disappeared.

Finally I got it, the reason why past lives were so well worth delving into, beyond their proving that our spirits survive death and that we really are eternal beings: by remembering and revealing the source of many seemingly inexplicable physical, mental, and emotional challenges, we can be healed.

I found that realization thrilling when the "lightbulb" first clicked on for me in the 1970s. I couldn't wait to share it with my close colleagues in the medical and psychiatric communities, all of whom were as intrigued as I was by anything and everything about reincarnation, from whether or not it existed to its potential significance. By then there was enough public interest in the idea of past lives and the soul's survival that, when my colleagues and I decided to conduct a weekend-long seminar to discuss it and exchange ideas, we found ourselves blessed with a standing-room-only crowd numbering in the hundreds.

I was eager to demonstrate a live past-life regression to this enthusiastic crowd. If it didn't work, oh well. If it did, how exciting for everyone in that auditorium, including my colleagues, who were as curious as the audience to see it. I asked for a volunteer and chose the least enthusiastic of the many people who had raised their hands—the last thing I wanted was an attention junkie who was simply leaping at the chance to show off. The attractive, well-dressed, rather shy man I chose looked as if he were curious but also wondering if he should have opted for going to a movie that day instead—in other words, an open-minded skeptic, my favorite kind of volunteer. His name was Paul, and after a brief explanation to him and the audience of what to expect during the hypnosis process, I asked him if there were any physical or emotional problems he'd like to address while he was under. He mentioned two:

a recurring pain in his right foot, which had never been properly diagnosed despite more trips to more podiatrists than he could count, and a lifelong belief that no matter how outwardly successful he might appear to be, he was simply disguising the fact that he was, in fact, inadequate and destined to be a disappointment to those who loved and counted on him. He'd worked with a couple of highly respected psychologists in an effort to overcome these feelings, but therapy had never seemed to produce lasting results.

His honesty was touching, apparent, and admirable, which I deeply appreciated. It was obvious to me and to the audience that he would tell the truth no matter what happened on that stage, even if, in the end, he found me and this whole regression thing to be as phony as a two-dollar bill.

He was responsive and easy to hypnotize. As always during regressive hypnosis, I gently guided him back through this life, his death in a previous life, and then into the heart of that life itself, at which moment he slumped and seemed to shrink into his chair, and his right foot twisted and turned in.

The life he described in great detail took place on a Virginia farm in 1821. Born with a clubfoot, he had been more of a burden than a help to his parents and mercilessly teased or completely ignored by his schoolmates.

As a result, he had been unable to make friends, no matter how hard he'd tried and through no fault of his own. He had died of pneumonia at the age of fifteen.

I eased him back to the present and, before I woke him, added a prayer in the form of a posthypnotic suggestion, which I used to end every past-life regression from that day forward: "And whatever pain or fear or negativity you might have carried over from a past life, release it and let it be resolved in the white light of the Holy Spirit. We ask this in the name of our Lord and the Mother and Father God, amen."

Paul left the stage looking "normal" again, if a little dazed, and he reported several weeks later that not only had the pain in his foot never returned but he'd also, for the first time in his life, begun to experience a peaceful sense of self-confidence and worthiness, which he'd never dreamed were within his reach.

One of the points I think I had trouble understanding about past lives before I began studying them was a basic principle that confuses a lot of people: basically, that a *past* life isn't *someone else's* life. Each of us has a spirit of our own, utterly unique and divine, and that spirit inhabits a variety of personas throughout a variety of incarnations. Whoever we are right this minute is a sum total of the wisdom and experience our spirit has gained during the lives it's lived before, both here and on the Other Side. We were no more some other person in any of our past lives than we were some other person when we were in diapers, or in first grade, or when we graduated from high school, or on the first day of our first job. Again, *think*. Without those cumulative experiences, whether we consciously remember them or not, we'd be un-potty-trained, uneducated, and unemployed.

Past lives work exactly the same logical way. If some other spirit than our own lived and learned from those lives, those lives would have no purpose. They're all ours, for better and worse, to enrich us and challenge us and add more steps along our eternal journey toward our own singular definition of perfection. Whoever you've been since time began and wherever your passions lie on the Other Side, where you live your *real* life, are all a part of who you are right now, whether or not you're consciously aware of your wealth of accumulated knowledge. Your spirit is holding it safe for you and sharing it with you when you open your mind, open your heart, and take the time and prayer to access it.

Remember, God created an orderly universe. There's nothing haphazard about anything that came from Him, including the amazing mechanisms that are our bodies and our minds. Things don't happen without a good, sound explanation. And there's a good, sound explanation for why our bodies and minds react to what's happened to us in lives that we've lived before. That reason is a phenomenon called cell memory.

I've written about cell memory in depth many times before, so I'll simply offer the abbreviated explanation here: The cells that make up our physical bodies are living, thinking, feeling organisms, which react with literal precision to the information they receive from our subconscious minds, where our spirit minds live and hold every moment and every memory of every one of our past lives. When our spirit minds enter our bodies for another incarnation, they infuse every cell with all the knowledge they possess, and the cells react in very real ways, with or without the participation of our conscious minds. It's as if our spirits say, "Oh, look, I'm inhabiting a human body again. I remember how this goes." By accessing those cell memories and shining the light of conscious awareness on them, we can rid ourselves of all the negativity our spirits have retained from the past and embrace all the joy, love, talent, interests, and overall health we've ever known.

I'll always be grateful to friends in the medical community who've been open-minded enough to suspend their skepticism about cell memory and give me a call when they've found themselves facing a physiological challenge that they can't seem to solve on their own.

For the most part they agree with my belief that, if it works, no matter how outlandish it might seem, it's worth a try—if and only if it's risk-free and consistent with the first tenet of the Hippocratic oath by which my licensed physician colleagues conduct their professional lives: first, do no harm.

I've never forgotten my first case, even though it seems like a thousand years ago instead of just forty. A surgeon at a veteran's hospital had been treating a patient named Randy, who'd suffered a debilitating back injury. After more than a dozen operations and countless hours of physical therapy, Randy was still in such excruciating pain that he'd been begging his doctors, including the one who called me, to sever his spinal cord. He'd been told in no uncertain terms that it would paralyze him and possibly even kill him, but by then either of those options sounded preferable to one more minute of the unbearable pain he simply couldn't endure any longer. My surgeon friend was desperate to avoid such a drastic solution—so desperate that he was willing to invite me to put my cell-memory theory to the test through regressive hypnosis and let the chips fall where they may.

I don't cry often, but I had to fight back tears when I met Randy in his hospital room. His eyes were dull and sunken from suffering too much pain for far too long, and his face was lifelessly gray. It touched me that his manners were still intact—he whispered, "Thank you for coming," when I came close to him to introduce myself and explain why I was there.

He slipped easily into deep hypnosis, and during our hour together he told me in a quiet, relaxed voice about two very relevant past lives.

The first was in Spain in the early 1700s. Randy, whose name was Paolo then, was deeply in love with a pretty, petite, dark-eyed twenty-two-year-old woman named Cristina. Unfortunately, Cristina happened to be married to Paolo's older brother, Caton. One night, when Paolo was on his way home from a tryst with Cristina, Caton ambushed him, buried an ax in his back, and left him on a rough dirt road to bleed out in the darkness.

Next came a much less dramatic life in central Georgia in the mid-1800s. Randy was Thomas then, a happy churchgoing farmer with a wife and four sons, around whom his whole world revolved. Thomas had just turned thirty-eight when he was painting his parents' two-story house and the ladder collapsed. His back was broken, paralyzing him from the chest down, and he died three months later.

An ax buried in his spine in one life, a broken back in a subsequent life, and a devastating, seemingly incurable back problem in this life. I refused then and I refuse now to believe it's coincidental, but of course it remained to be seen what effect, if any, Randy's unearthing of these past-life injuries would have on the extreme situation in which I'd found him. Before I brought him out from under hypnosis, I prayed for him to release those long-ago wounds into the white light of the Holy Spirit, so that he could let go of his cell-memory belief that inhabiting a body meant back injuries and that back injuries inevitably resulted in death.

Three weeks later Randy's surgeon called with an update. After his session with me, Randy had never again asked that his spine be severed. He'd even insisted on being helped out of bed and, for the first time in months, had taken some tentative but proud steps up and down the hospital corridors with the help of a walker, to the amazement and applause of the staff. His prognosis had improved enormously, and both he and his surgeon felt as if a miracle had taken place.

That phone call ended with an exclamation I've been hearing ever since, after virtually every client's hypnosis-induced cell-memory experience: "I don't know what you did or how you did it, but it worked." My reply was exactly the same then as it is now: "It's not me. It's God and my past-live regression subjects.

I just clear the path for their spirit minds to uncover the real source of their pain so the wounds can heal."

And in case you're wondering how legitimate the idea is of our cells being infused with information beyond our very limited experience in this life alone, let me share a story that found its way to me when I'd just begun exploring the subject, an extraordinary story that demonstrated a whole new twist on cell memory and its power.

Grace was in her early fifties, and she'd just undergone a successful kidney transplant, performed by a surgeon friend of mine. Grace had never smoked in her life or touched even a sip of alcohol, so imagine her shock when she awoke from surgery wanting nothing more on this earth than a cigarette and an extra-dry martini. The kidney donor's family was almost as shocked as Grace—cigarettes and martinis had been two of the donor's greatest passions. With just a couple of hypnosis sessions performed during Grace's recovery, I was able to help Grace's subconscious mind separate the "foreign" cell memories of her new kidney from the cells of her own body and recognize that those cravings were neither real nor relevant.

Cell memory passed from an organ donor to a recipient is becoming an acknowledged and widely studied phenomenon in the medical community. A fairly recent and unforgettable case in point was told to me a few years ago by the late Dr. Paul Pearsall, a renowned Hawaiian psychoneuroimmunologist, clinical and educational psychologist, and author.

It began with the unspeakable murder of a ten-year-old girl, a murder that was unsolved and in danger of going cold. The one glimmer of joy in this obscene tragedy was that the ten-year-old victim was a compatible donor for an eight-year-old girl who was in desperate need of a heart transplant.

The transplant went perfectly, and the eight-year-old was on the road to a complete recovery and a long, healthy life when she began suffering from terrifying nightmares of her donor's murder and the man who had committed it. The recurring dreams were so disturbing that the girl's deeply concerned mother sought the help of a pediatric psychiatrist.

As the sessions progressed and the little girl's memories of her nightmares became more and more clear, some very specific details about the murderer emerged, details so specific about his eyes, his hands, and his teeth, in particular, that the psychiatrist and the girl's mother felt compelled to contact the police.

I would love to have seen the look on the detective's face while he listened to the answer to his understandable question, "Where did you get this information?"

But to his credit, he didn't dismiss it. A cold case is a cold case, after all, and he was in no position to ignore a lead, no matter how unlikely its source.

He methodically set about investigating everything the eight-year-old girl had reported from her nightmares, including a detailed composite drawing of the suspect done by a police sketch artist, based on the child's description. A few months later, based on nothing but the cell memories infused in the girl by her heart donor, the detective arrested a man who eventually pleaded guilty before going to trial. A murderer was off the streets, and the miracle of cell memory was proven one more time.

Another colleague of mine, a neurologist with a quick, inquisitive mind and a rabid curiosity about reincarnation, came up with an interesting angle I might never have thought of on my own. He wondered if birthmarks, instead of being random pigmentation irregularities, could have some connection to past lives, and he asked if I would conduct my own casual survey on that subject among my hypnotic regression clients. Far be it from me to say no to a friend, especially if there might be something interesting to learn from saying yes and no potential harm in trying.

The same day he asked, a client named Joey came in for a past-life regression, curious to know whom in his present life he'd known before. In the course of his session he talked with great passion about his life as an Algonquin Indian in the early 1800s, a life that had ended when he was twenty-two from a knife wound to his right leg, just below the knee. Before he left my office, I casually asked if he happened to have any birthmarks. Only one, he said almost apologetically, as if he thought that he might be disappointing me, and he rolled up his pant leg to show me an angry-looking, purplish discoloration about two inches below his right knee. Since he had no memory of what he'd told me during his regression, he had no idea why I was so fascinated by it, nor did I tell him. I just thanked him and wished him well, made a note to mention it to my neurologist friend, and frankly wrote it off as an interesting fluke.

Several hundred past-life regressions and almost that many birthmarks later, I realized it was far too much of a coincidence to write off. In fact, the final tally when I stopped keeping track was that 90 percent of my clients had birthmarks precisely where past-life wounds had been inflicted. And the more I thought about it, the more sense it made. Since the spirit enters the body with clear memories of the major traumas and injuries it experienced in previous bodies, why wouldn't the cells of the new body form physical evidence of those past injuries, like scars from another lifetime?

So, if you happen to have a birthmark, don't give it a second thought, if that's what makes you comfortable. Or, if you enjoy opening your mind to a whole new world of fascinating possibilities, ask yourself if you might be looking at physical proof of your own sacred, thrilling immortality.

Yet another twist on cell memory, which I never would have thought of on my own, was inadvertently introduced to me by a client named Mike. He had come in not for a past-life regression but for what he described as "something that's really shaken me up, but there's no one else I can talk to about it because they'll think I'm crazy." Needless to say, after the life I've lived and the number of times that adjective has been used on me, I'm not about to accuse anyone of being crazy.

Mike and his wife had returned a month earlier from a trip to London, a place he'd always longed to visit "although I have no idea why." He'd done no research in anticipation of the trip; he'd just reserved a room at a well-known hotel and tickets for a couple of popular plays and for a tour of the city on their first day there.

"We were only a few minutes into the tour when the oddest feeling came over me, that this place I'd never been before felt awfully familiar. And as impossible as it seemed, I actually began to recognize where I was. We turned a corner and I thought, 'We're about to pass St. Paul's Cathedral,' and sure enough, there it was. I'd think, 'Scotland Yard is just ahead on our right,' and seconds later the tour guide would point out Scotland Yard through the loudspeaker. This kind of thing went on for the whole two weeks we were in England. One day we rented a car to go for a drive in the countryside, and we came upon a small house that I knew used to be a pub. In fact, the words 'my favorite pub is gone' hit me so strongly that they almost came out of my mouth, but I didn't want my wife to start worrying about my sanity and fly home without me. I did ask about it in the nearby village, though, and I was right—the house had been converted from a pub about three generations earlier. So please, tell me the truth. What's going on? How could that happen? Am I psychic, or nuts, or both?"

The answer, of course, was neither. My Spirit Guide, Francine, gave me the in-depth explanation: Mike had experienced a classic example of yet another result of cell memory called morphic resonance. It occurs when the spirit encounters a place or person or circumstance so familiar from a past life that it infuses the conscious mind with a sense of familiarity and even homesickness.

Mike and I ended up doing a regressive hypnosis session the day he came to see me. He described not one but two happy lifetimes in London, and he'd owned the small fieldstone pub in the north countryside in one of those lifetimes. The overwhelming feeling of recognition is no different really than a memory you might have of your childhood home, or a beloved vacation spot, or a dear friend from grade school you haven't seen in a very long time. Remember, we're not different people in our past lives. We're the same person, the same spirit we always were and always will be, and many of the cell memories we carry with us are sweet, reassuring, and worth cherishing.

Even if you haven't experienced morphic resonance about a certain place, I'm willing to bet that you've experienced it about the people in your life. As a casual mental exercise, and don't think too hard about it, let your mind wander, one at a time, through your friends, your family, your coworkers, and even those acquaintances you keep at arm's length because the two of you don't particularly like each other. Now I want you to ask yourself the simple question, "Have I known this person before?" You'll be fascinated by how easily you're able to answer that question with an immediate yes or no about everyone you know.

Perhaps the most important thing for you to know about past lives—beyond the fact that you are the sum total of every life you've lived before, both on earth and on the Other Side, where our *real* lives, our real joy, our real growth takes place—is that each and every one of them is the result of our own design.

I've written at length about charts in other books, including my most recent, *Afterlives of the Rich and Famous,* so I'll just offer an overview here to help the celebrity past lives that you're about to read make even more sense to you: You are here by choice, on a brief trip away from Home, to further the progress of your soul on an eternal journey toward the greatest perfection you can achieve. When you decide that you have more to learn and accomplish, you come here to attend the roughest school there is. An obvious question is: "If the Other Side is so blissful, and my life there is so idyllic, why would I ever leave it once I was there?" The answer can be summed up with another question: "What have you learned when times were good?"

It's a genetic legacy from our Creator, throughout the eternity He promised us, that we're constantly yearning to be better, wiser, more loving, more giving, and more productive in order to achieve whatever our own greatest potential happens to be. While a lot can be learned from the endless research sources and the other spirits with whom we spend our time and share our lives at Home, there are many lessons that can only be learned from hands-on experience. How can you know how good an artist you can be if you've read a thousand art books and visited a thousand museums but never picked up a paintbrush? How do you know how accomplished a pianist you can be if you've studied the compositions of the most brilliant composers in history and traveled the world attending performances of the best of the best but never touched a keyboard? And following that logic, how can you know how courageous you are until you've faced fear? How can you know how strong your faith is, in yourself and in your God, until you've faced negativity and godlessness?

Since there's no fear, negativity, or godlessness on the Other Side, we make the choice from time to time, for our own spiritual progress, to come to earth, where those challenges are inescapable. And before we leave Home, each of us composes meticulously detailed charts for our upcoming incarnations to make sure we accomplish the goals that brought us here in the first place.

We design literally every aspect of our lives: our families, our friends, our enemies, our victories, our disappointments, our crises, our illnesses, our careers, our hobbies—every aspect. Not one of us designs a perfect lifetime. If perfection were what we were after, we wouldn't opt to come here in the first place. In fact, writing our charts in an atmosphere of perfection often causes us to overreach and design more challenges than we can handle, no different than walking into a grocery store when you're hungry and finding yourself tempted to say, "One of each, please." I've thought to myself a million times, as you may have too, that I must have been drunk when I wrote my chart—it's the only possible explanation for my having thought every moment of this lifetime was a good idea.

Fortunately, the process of incarnating and planning our upcoming lifetimes includes a series of safeguards so that we don't get too carried away. The saying "God doesn't give us anything we can't handle" could be accurately reworded to read, "God doesn't let us chart anything we can't handle in any given incarnation." Our souls learn based on our capacity to understand the lessons, and that capacity is based on our education and experience. Just as we would never expect a kindergarten student to tackle an exam on aerospace engineering—or to benefit from trying—God, who knows the progress of our souls far better than we do, will never burden us with "aerospace engineering" until we've passed the "courses" required to master it, no matter how few or how many lifetimes that takes.

Bear in mind that we write our charts on the Other Side, where memories of our past lives are completely intact. (On the off chance that we need help remembering, every chart of every lifetime we've lived is carefully preserved on parchment scrolls in the magnificent Hall of Records, one of the first buildings we see when we return Home.) All that knowledge is taken into account as we design our upcoming incarnations, including the people we will meet along the way, from family members to friends to spouses to enemies. And if, by mutual agreement, we decide that it could be to our benefit to meet certain people again in the life we're about to experience—to befriend, to marry, to be part of our immediate family, or even to avoid like the plague—we and those significant people from past lives include each other in our charts, even designing when, where, and how we're going to find each other here on earth.

You'll read many examples of those past-life reunions in the stories that follow, and please don't think for a moment that there's anything accidental or coincidental about them.

Every celebrity in this book has lived many lives before the one they just left behind. You know their accomplishments while they were here among us, and you'll find that their previous incarnations led them, often in nonlinear ways, to the part of their spirit's journey for which they're best known.

But it's important before we begin that I explain the term "point of entry."

When I first began doing past-life regressions for clients, it was fascinating to listen to the breathless awe with which they found themselves actually experiencing their previous incarnations. When the novelty wore off, I realized that each regression could have gone on for hours or even days at a time. Don't get me wrong— every life, past or present, is interesting. But as you'll find as you read about the following celebrities, most of them, and most of us, have lived anywhere from fourteen to fifty-some past lives, not all of which are directly relevant to the most recent and famous incarnation. Some of my earliest clients would delight in wandering around from one life to another to another without ever getting to the life or lives or events that were causing a relevant cell-memory impact.

I like to use the relatable analogy of our school years from, let's say, kindergarten through twelfth grade. I'm sure I don't just speak for myself when I admit that I didn't exactly appreciate or retain every bit of information taught in every subject I took. I would often sit in my classes trying not to doze off and thinking, "What on earth do square roots, or the primary export of Brazil, or the number of teeth in the mouth of the average frog have to do with preparing me for my future?"

Looking back, I wasn't necessarily wrong; but while not every course ultimately proved useful in any literal way, together they added up to a well-rounded education and provided study disciplines that are still valuable to me every day of my life.

Many of our past lives are much like those supposedly irrelevant school subjects. They haven't all had an equal impact on who we are today. They haven't all been wildly significant or remarkable, nor did we design them to be. Add them up, though, and they're part of the sum total of where we each are at this moment in our soul's journey, essential to a well-rounded education and to the unique path we each chose for ourselves.

I finally had a talk with my Spirit Guide, Francine, and asked if there was a way to gently direct a client, without leading or offending them, to the incarnation(s) that reflected the subjects in which they intended to major, so to speak, or the cell-memory issues that were having the greatest impact on their current lives and with which they might be struggling.

"That's simple," she said. "Just tell them to go to the point of entry. They'll understand what it means."

I'd never heard of the point of entry, nor had any of my clients until they were under hypnosis. Then, at my suggestion that they go to the point of entry, their spirit jumped instantly to the lifetime in which the event or events happened that had created their most significant cell memories to begin with.

So, as you read about the following celebrities, you'll find that we only explore a tiny fraction of their total number of incarnations, and I want to be sure that you understand why. Like all of us, these celebrities studied many seemingly insignificant subjects along the way; not all of the subjects were worth mentioning but, in the end, they are all necessary stepping-stones on the paths of some truly unforgettable souls.

And, by the way, please don't think for a moment that these people are special just because they achieved celebrity status in their most recent lifetimes. You and they have the same Father and the same eternity in common, and I want these pages to be as much about you as they are about "the rich and famous." So I hope you'll enjoy their stories, dictated to me by my Spirit Guide, Francine. I hope just as much that, when you reach the end of the book, you'll both read and actually perform the three-part exercise there, as often as you like. Not only will you enjoy it, and not only will it relax you, but it will also give you peace, comfort, and joyful glimpses into your own sacred soul.

PART TWO
The Celebrities

ELIZABETH TAYLOR

Elizabeth Taylor was a complex woman who earned her complexity through forty-seven past lives, creating the celebrated movie star we knew and admired in her most recent lifetime. Three of those forty-seven lives had especially strong influences on the woman whose final incarnation ended on March 23, 2011.

The first of those three incarnations took place in Babylonia in the second century BC. Elizabeth's name was Anata, then, and she was a tall, regal, brown-skinned woman with dark almond-shaped eyes and straight black hair. Her father was a successful wheat farmer. The family's wealth and elevated social status allowed them frequent access to royalty, and at the age of fifteen she married a Babylonian prince, who introduced her to the concept of deities and gods whose powers were far greater than those of mortal men. She became deeply religious, a devoted student and practitioner of Babylonian theology, and she raised her four children with a strong foundation of faith.

Her husband died of pleurisy when Anata was seventy-three. Her children had long since left home, and she spent the remaining two years of her life in solitary prayer and meditation. Her death in that life was the result of a broken back, which had immobilized her when she was alone in her house, so for days her body lay undiscovered on the floor near a statue of the goddess Hera.

The next dramatically relevant incarnation on the journey of Elizabeth's soul was during the 1500s, when she chose a lifetime as the abbess of a Benedictine convent in Switzerland. Her name was Marie Lilliane, and her introduction to the convent was heartbreaking. Because her parents were too self-centered and hedonistic to have any interest in or responsibility for their child, they abandoned her at the abbey when she was twelve years old. She'd become monotheistic since her incarnation in Babylonia and had chosen to forfeit a secular life to focus solely on her commitment to God. Her eventual elevation to the role of abbess was an acknowledgment of that devout commitment.

Marie Lilliane was refreshingly lenient with the nuns in her care, not forcing rigid rules or schedules on them behind the high stone convent walls but insisting that they dress and behave with utmost propriety in public. She also insisted that they follow her example of ministering every day to the spiritual needs of the elderly, the orphans, and the stray animals in the village near the convent.

She died of pneumonia at the age of eighty-nine, believing that even after a lifetime of godliness and caring for those who couldn't care for themselves, she hadn't done enough or been reverent enough to deserve an eternity in the immediate presence of God on the Other Side. She couldn't have been more surprised, relieved, and humbled to find herself emerging from the legendary tunnel into the waiting arms of her loved ones at Home.

When she began her next life, in France in the 1700s, she overcompensated for her virtually cloistered incarnation in the Swiss convent, which had left her still feeling inadequate. Instead, this time around she chose an exclusively secular, self-involved life. Her name was Chantell, and she was a legendarily beautiful, seductive courtesan who demanded, and received, an enormous amount of attention. She was adored and supported by two members of Marie Antoinette's inner circle, who knew about each other but adored her too much to risk losing her by demanding that she choose between them. One of those men was a notoriously wild and adventurous nobleman named François, whom she found to be a stimulating challenge. The other was Arnaud, a member of the French aristocracy, known to be brilliant, intense, and brooding, and to possess a quick, explosive temper. Chantell loved him deeply, almost to the point of addiction, and believed him when he repeatedly told her that their hours together gave him the only happiness he knew in an otherwise hollow life troubled by periods of both excessive euphoria and intense darkness, which we would today call bipolar disorder. Her heart belonged to him even though all logic accurately told her that there was no future for the two of them.

Several incarnations later, François would be known as Mike Todd, Elizabeth Taylor's third husband. Arnaud married Chantell not once but twice during his most recent lifetime as Richard Burton.

Chantell had great wealth, physical beauty, a spectacular mansion with servants she hired and fired at will, and her choice of the most desirable men in all of France. But when her beauty began to fade, the men began to move on to younger women. Eventually Chantell had no money with which to employ servants, maintain her mansion, or care for the only souls she truly loved in that life, the dogs and cats of all breeds and sizes that had their run of her estate. Without her beauty and the slavish adoration of the men around her, she felt she had no value. She wanted nothing more than to hide and be left alone. At the age of fifty-four, she died in her crumbling mansion, lonely and destitute, of peritonitis from a burst appendix.

In her latest and last life, Elizabeth Taylor finally found the balance she'd been seeking between the spiritual and the secular. Her beauty was still legendary, but she used it well, as an actress and a businesswoman, to earn her own fortune and to not be dependent on anyone but herself. She had many lovers and husbands, made her share of mistakes, and lived a life many might consider excessive, but she was also a fiercely loyal and generous friend. Her ongoing health problems proved to be amazing examples of cell memory in action. She fought them and bore them bravely. And her conversion to Judaism was the manifestation of a yearning in her life for a formalized religion and a joyful recognition that the earthly steps of her spiritual journey were finally complete. She went Home on March 23, 2011.

MICHAEL JACKSON

Michael Jackson was a young soul, with only nine incarnations on this earth, and the lifetime that ended in 2009 will be his last. One of the most remarkable aspects of his past lives—and I've never seen this in all my years of doing regressions and consulting with my Spirit Guide, Francine, about specific people's histories—is that Michael's ninth and final incarnation was the only one in which he lived past the age of fourteen. For everyone who's ever wondered why he seemed so much more comfortable with children than adults, now you know. And let me stress something with absolute certainty: he was not a pedophile. Not once, not ever, and it's tragic that he was misunderstood enough to even be accused of such a thing. As for his passionate, lifelong involvement with children's charities, I should add that seven of his lives were spent in poverty—three in Africa, one in El Salvador, two in the Middle East, and one in the Appalachian mountains of the United States. He ached for starving, impoverished children because he was one, over and over again.

But there's no doubt that the point-of-entry incarnation that most dramatically shaped the extraordinary lifetime of the superstar we knew as Michael Jackson took place in Burma, about a century before Christ was born. His name, as best I can make it out from Francine's high-pitched chirping, was Tha. He was born prematurely and weighed just over three pounds at birth. His beautiful young mother was very ill and depressed after delivering her first and only baby and traveled home to her parents in India to recuperate, leaving Tha in the care of his father and a live-in nurse.

Tha's father was a member of the king's court, and a loyal and trusted aide. Rarely has a father adored his son more or been more sensitive to the emotional and physical fragility into which Tha was born. Tha was a sweet, happy, introverted child, curious and funny and intensely respectful. In fact, the first time Tha, at the age of three, was presented to the king, after a lot of coaching from his father, he genuflected so deeply and for so long that the king began to wonder if the boy had fallen asleep.

Tha was four when his father and a group of friends took him on a hunting trip. On the first day, Tha's father was excited to have killed a tiger, until his son let out an agonized scream, raced to the dead animal, and threw himself on top of its carcass, sobbing and asking his father over and over again, "How could you? He did nothing to you. How could you kill him?" His father, surprised and deeply saddened by his son's despair, held him and promised he would never hunt again. He kept that promise for the rest of his life.

They had barely returned from the hunting trip when Tha developed a fever and his skin broke out in a painful rash and blisters. At first his father had thought it might have been a reaction to the trauma his son had suffered on the death of the tiger, but finally the king's finest physicians were summoned to examine the boy. Their conclusion was that Tha, with an already compromised immune system from his premature birth, was severely allergic to the sun. From that day forward Tha never set foot outside the house, and his environment was kept as dark and sterile as possible to prevent any further inadvertent threats to his health.

The great delight in Tha's life was one of his father's skills, which had also proved to be invaluable in the king's court: Tha's father was a brilliant puppeteer. He'd created an amazing collection of hand-carved marionettes, to which he was constantly adding, and Tha proved to be gifted as well at the intricate carving and painting required to give each of them a distinct personality.

The marionettes served a far greater purpose than that of simple entertainment. They were also used as a kind of liaison between the king and his subjects. When the king had news or an edict to announce to the public that he thought might be unpopular, he dispatched Tha's father and the marionettes to perform the announcements, which helped to soften the blow and separate the king from his subjects' disfavor. And when there was news or a message from the people that might displease the king, the marionettes were the perfect buffers against any initial rage he was likely to inflict on a living messenger.

The marionettes mesmerized Tha. He loved carving and painting their intricate faces. He loved designing costumes for them for his father to sew. He loved watching his father rehearse with them for upcoming appearances. But most of all, he loved duplicating their every move, from their lively dances to their oddly stiff but graceful ways of greeting and interacting with each other. He was brilliant at it and would practice for hours, watching his reflection in the windows of the house to make sure that even the slightest gestures and steps were perfect. His father was in awe of his talent, and he treasured the private recitals Tha performed just for him every night after they'd finished their dinner. Sadly, no one but Tha's father ever saw those performances; he would have proudly had his son dance for the king, but Tha was too shy to even consider such a thing. His father, always respectful of his beloved son's sensitivities, never forced the issue and remained the only person to be blessed with a "preview" of the extraordinary entertainer we knew as Michael Jackson.

Tha's lifetime in ancient Burma ended when his immune deficiencies finally caught up with him. He died of complications from pneumonia at the age of thirteen. His father never recovered from the death of his son. But Tha, when he arrived at Home, was overjoyed to be greeted by his mother, the woman who had ultimately died giving birth to him.

By the way, no one from that lifetime accompanied Michael Jackson into his final incarnation.

MOTHER TERESA

Agnes Gonxha Bojaxhiu, who came to be known as Mother Teresa in her fifty-fourth and final incarnation, is obviously a rare, incredibly advanced spirit.

Unlike the vast majority of us, who continue returning to earth for the growth of our own souls, she continued to return for the sake of others, always feeling that her work on earth was incomplete as long as there was still poverty, hunger, and suffering in this world.

Among her first incarnations was a life as a woman named Leah during the time of Christ. She knew him through her lifelong friendship with the apostle Luke. She followed him and she cherished her association with him, always staying in the background and feeling unworthy to be in his presence but promising herself and God that she would devote her life to his teachings. She was at the Sermon on the Mount, which elevated her spirit for an eternity, and from a distance, as her heart broke, she witnessed the crucifixion.

Filled with the Holy Spirit and committed to her promise to God, she began traveling the countryside around Jerusalem, administering the sacraments and spreading the word of Christ throughout the small villages there, humbly receiving food and a place to sleep in exchange. Even though she was not affiliated with any formal order or church, the religious leaders of the time, patriarchal as they were, became aware of her and demanded that she stop her work immediately or face imprisonment.

Being asked to stop her work was like being asked to stop breathing, as far as she was concerned. Instead, she simply left the area and traveled to Haifa and to Jordan, where she continued to offer Communion, share Christ's word, pray with those in need, and tend to the sick and bereaved. She was called Beloved Sister and developed a small following of her own, but she insisted that no one follow her without working side by side with her and that their adoration be reserved solely for Christ, not for her.

She also founded a number of modest hospices along the way and taught several of her followers to administer last rites and counsel grieving families about eternal life, the resurrection, the survival of the soul, and the joyful peace that awaited their loved ones in God's arms on the Other Side.

As her small following grew, so did the danger of her being tracked by the men who'd threatened to punish her if she continued her work. She was eventually arrested in Haifa for crimes against the church and returned to Jerusalem, where she was imprisoned until she died at the age of ninety-one. The good works she did along the way remained and continued to offer hope, solace, healing, and Christ's lessons to those whose lives she'd touched, and she went Home with a grateful heart.

In a subsequent life in the 1800s, she returned as a Hawaiian woman named Hani. She lived on the island of Molokai with her devoutly Catholic parents, both of whom worked on a nearby sugarcane plantation. She was only seventeen when she tragically contracted leprosy and was banished to the leper colony on the island, shortly after Father Damien had arrived there. She became one of his most devoted followers and helpers for as long as her illness allowed, taking care of others before she'd allow her own needs to be tended to.

A ship regularly sailed past the colony bearing a priest who wouldn't set foot on land inhabited by a leper colony. It became a tradition for Father Damien and Hani to stand side by side on the shore, as close to the ship as they could get, and shout their confessions to the priest. She was in awe of Father Damien and his compassionate, selfless, life-threatening work in the colony, and he was equally in awe of her and her refusal to let her fatal illness keep her from losing her faith or her desire to be of whatever help she could.

Father Damien typically began his sermons with the words, "You dear lepers . . ." One day, to everyone's profound shock, he began his sermon by saying, "We lepers . . ." Like everyone else, Hani was devastated and never left Father Damien's side as leprosy overtook his body. Even though she was far more ill than he was, she saw to it that he ate, she bandaged his sores, and she sat by his bedside, reading his favorite Bible passages aloud until he fell asleep.

Her death preceded his by more than a year, and while many others were there to care for him, he missed her every day until he too died of leprosy. She was among the first to greet him when he returned to the Other Side, and he proudly agreed to be her Spirit Guide when she decided to incarnate for the last time in the beatified life she lived as Mother Teresa.

JOHN WAYNE

John Wayne's incarnation as one of the most successful movie stars in history was affected in many ways by the thirty-four lifetimes that preceded it. He lived twelve of those lifetimes in Spain or Mexico, which explains his well-established deep attraction to Latina women in his most recent incarnation, three of whom he married. But other facets of his past lives affected him more subtly.

One of his several lifetimes in Spain took place in the 1500s. His name was Juan Carlos, and from early childhood he was uncommonly handsome, attracting attention everywhere he went. His parents were unapologetic opportunists. His mother was the family breadwinner, a fortune-teller with a widespread following, famous for removing curses and casting spells for a great deal of money—money which both parents spent as quickly and ostentatiously as possible.

Juan Carlos's mother recognized her beautiful son's potential as another source of income almost as soon as he took his first baby steps. Through her many clients, she arranged for him to learn all the social graces and refined tastes of the moneyed elite. As he grew more and more handsome, he also developed impeccable manners, highly polished charm, and a vast knowledge of art, opera, wine, literature, and architecture. He learned to be an accomplished equestrian and polo player. By the time he was sixteen, his looks and his carefully cultivated sophistication had made him a source of intense interest among wealthy men and women alike.

It wasn't long before all the efforts of Juan Carlos and his mother began to pay off. In addition to becoming a rather renowned model for painters and sculptors throughout Spain, Portugal, and France, he also became a prized escort for some of Madrid's wealthiest women, who competed for his attention with money, gifts, and discreetly located, well-appointed homes. Juan Carlos was only too happy to share his great good fortune with his parents, who, as they'd done with their own money, spent every coin he gave them and never hesitated to demand more. Because of them, and despite his beautiful homes, impeccable wardrobe, and countless possessions, Juan Carlos was often broke, at least until his ardently devoted lovers provided him with a fresh supply of cash.

Unfortunately, the husband of one of his wealthiest "patrons" had discovered where his wife and much of his money were perpetually disappearing. He also happened to be politically powerful. So, when the time came for the Spanish armada to set sail for England, Juan Carlos was kidnapped and held captive on one of the ships. That ship was destroyed in a massive burst of flames.

It was both good news and bad news that Juan Carlos survived the fire. He returned to Madrid alive, but his face was horribly disfigured and one of his legs had been amputated. His parents, deprived of their source of income and having no idea where their son had gone, had long since fled to live with relatives in Italy, where his mother resumed her fortune-telling practice. Because he was no longer handsome or physically fit, Juan Carlos was of no further use or interest to his wealthy admirers, who had thought he'd abandoned them when he'd been kidnapped. He was now homeless, unemployable, and in severe physical and psychological pain, having been transformed from a man who had been universally admired to a man from whom people turned away in revulsion.

At the age of twenty-six, Juan Carlos hanged himself from a tree on the estate of one of his former lovers and her husband, the man who'd taken him away against his will and destroyed his life.

It was a well-publicized source of conflict and regret in John Wayne's life that, while he was without question a patriot and a courageous, honorable man, he passively evaded serving in the military and watched fellow actors, colleagues, and friends march off to war. Wouldn't it be interesting to know what would have happened if he'd been able to restore his conscious memory of that past life in which war had become synonymous with irretrievably losing everything rather than have the cell memory of it paralyze him with such seemingly unexplained guilt?

He had an infinitely happier incarnation in the early 1800s. His name was Albert, and he was one of four sons born to a logger and his wife in a small town in Georgia. A bright, interested student, he grew up to find a combination of careers that suited him perfectly: he became a trusted and popular veterinarian and a blacksmith. It was on his professional travels throughout the state that he met and fell in love with a fascinating woman named

Eva. She'd been a well-known Shakespearean actress in England until a scandal had prompted her to move to the United States to start a new life with the by-product of that scandal, a lovely three-year-old daughter.

Albert and Eva married soon after meeting, and he built a handsome fieldstone house for his new wife and much-adored child on the outskirts of the small town where his parents and brothers still lived. He focused his practices closer to home, still bringing in a handsome income and being an excellent provider. He and Eva gave Eva's daughter five younger sisters, and theirs was a busy, happy household.

When the Georgia gold rush hit just a few miles from home, Albert was one of its first and most fortunate participants, becoming extremely wealthy in just a few short years. It was neither his dream nor his nature to become a man of leisure, and he continued his veterinary and blacksmithing practices out of love for and loyalty to his clients and their animals. But he was also able to build a small theater in town where his wife could return to the stage, as she'd been yearning to do. After a lot of coaching and rehearsing, Albert and Eva actually appeared in several Shakespearean plays together, recruiting talent from around the South and creating a popular venue that lasted until it was destroyed by fire in the 1870s. Albert found acting to be an exciting new skill and a stimulating mental exercise that he thoroughly enjoyed. And thanks to Eva's expert teaching, he became very good at it.

Albert was seventy-four when he died of lung disease in that life. His wife, daughters, and twenty-six grandchildren were with him when he passed away in the house that he had built, smiling with great contentment as he took his last breath.

It's probably worth noting that the gold rush that helped make Albert his fortune began at a place called Duke's Creek, which could easily be why he always found that nickname so appealing in his most recent incarnation. He'll be back for one more lifetime.

DONNA REED

The ultimate girl next door and the ideal TV mom and homemaker, the wholesome warmth that made Donna Reed a star on both big and small screens came naturally to her from many of her thirty-nine lives. She's completed the earthly part of her soul's journey and has been happily back at work as an Orientator on the Other Side since she returned there in 1986.

Odd as it may seem, one of her most beloved incarnations was spent as a slave, a terrified thirteen-year-old named Olatunde, who was transported from Africa to Virginia in the mid-1600s. In an eerie bit of foreshadowing, she was one of a small group made to wait for the next transport because the ship on which they were supposed to sail was too crowded to accommodate them. The ship they missed was hit by a fierce storm in the middle of the Atlantic, and everyone on board drowned as the ship sank. (Hundreds of years later, Donna Reed was scheduled on a flight from Texas to Burbank, but the flight was overbooked, so she was rescheduled to take the next plane. The plane she missed crashed on its approach to the Burbank airport, killing everyone on board.)

Once she arrived in America, Olatunde was promptly sold to a Virginia tobacco plantation owner and his wife. They changed her name to Victoria and settled her into the maids' quarters in their mansion. Slowly but surely she began to realize that they meant her no harm, that they actually intended to be kind to her. They hired a tutor to teach her to speak, read, and write English. And while they expected her to work very hard, they also insisted that she adhere to an early bedtime appropriate to a teenager. She didn't understand the ramifications at the time, but they entered into a contract with her that essentially made her an indentured servant rather than a slave, so once she had fulfilled her ten-year contract, she would be free—with the one condition that she becomes a Christian.

Victoria attended church with her new "masters," and it was like nourishment to a starving soul. She'd been raised in the poverty of a primitive, isolated village in which the only priority was basic day-to-day survival, so she'd never been exposed to such magnificent concepts as a loving God and His son Jesus Christ, who'd died and been resurrected for the insignificant likes of her. Not only did she thrive in the joy of her newfound religion, she also lent her amazing singing voice to the performance of hymns, which elevated the spirits of the whole congregation and made her "masters" proud.

Victoria was a smart girl and a quick learner. The family housekeeper taught her every facet of maintaining a beautiful home: cleaning, cooking, laundry, setting a perfect table, and keeping her mistress's wardrobe in perfect order and condition. (The observation that Donna Reed would have been proud is too irresistible to pass up.) And Victoria was part of the celebration when the news came that a baby would be joining the family in the next several months.

When Victoria was seventeen, a twenty-one-year-old slave named Barnard was purchased to work in the fields, a strong, handsome young man with the first green eyes she'd ever seen. They inevitably met and were immediately attracted to each other, and even though she knew it was wrong, Victoria began sneaking out of the house to be with him in the dark tobacco fields. His story broke her heart: he'd been torn away from his young wife and six-month-old son when he was fifteen and sold into slavery by a trader who'd promised that he could send for his family after he'd worked in America for a year. After that year, the trader and his promise were nowhere to be found, and Barnard had later learned that his wife had married another man and disappeared with their son, never to be seen again. Victoria wanted nothing more than to ease Barnard's grief, his simmering rage, and his lone-liness. She begged him to come to church with her, which he refused, but failing that, she spent every free moment with him.

Perhaps inevitably, she became pregnant. She was terrified to break the news to her owners and to her church pastor, but Barnard had a ready solution: through his connections, they could run away together and start a family, someplace they would never be found, and live off the wages she'd managed to save until those same connections provided him with another job on another plantation. Victoria was desperately torn. She was in love with Barnard and believed it would bring peace to his soul to have a new wife and child from whom he wouldn't be torn away again. But she also loved the man and woman for whom she worked, who'd treated her like a member of their family, introduced her to the sacred word of Christ and, not insignificantly, signed a contract with her, which indebted her to them for another six years.

It deeply disturbed her that Barnard didn't understand her dilemma. He'd expected an immediate yes from her, and he pressured her relentlessly. The stress of such a difficult decision, and of keeping such huge secrets from her owners and her church, caused her to miscarry in her fourth month. While she was devastated at the loss of her baby, she was also a bit relieved— now there would be no need for her and Barnard to run away. They could stay where they were, continuing their commitments to the plantation where they were both treated well, develop a proper, open relationship, and marry in an appropriate amount of time.

Barnard was having none of it. He still wanted her to run away with him and start a new life, with her savings to tide them over until he found work again. In the end, she refused. Her mistress's baby was due at any moment, and she knew she would never forgive herself if she abandoned her mistress and caused her the same kind of stress that had cost Victoria her child.

She begged Barnard to understand and be patient. She wasn't rejecting him, after all, and they could have a nice life together right where they were.

One morning they all woke to discover that Barnard was gone. He'd slipped away during the night, leaving none of his few belongings and no note to Victoria. She was devastated and, for comfort, immersed herself in her work, her church, and in the arrival of her owners' first child, a beautiful daughter whom they named Charlotte. The baby girl brought great joy to the household. Victoria delighted in helping care for her, and she felt privileged to be invited to her baptism.

The time came when Victoria had fully honored her contract and was free to set out on her own. The family wanted her to stay but assured her that they would understand if she preferred to leave. She very much wanted to stay, she told them, but first she felt she should tell them the truth about herself, since they might not think so highly of her or wish to continue her employment if they knew. Taking a deep breath, she told them everything about her relationship with Barnard, including his tragic history, his urging her to run away with him, and the miscarriage she'd suffered.

They couldn't have been more compassionate. They were terribly sad that she hadn't told them sooner, so that they could have helped her through such a terrible time, and they admired her enormously for being so honest when she thought it might cost her her job. They very much wanted her to stay. They trusted her more than ever and they were horrified to hear the tragic circumstances of Barnard being wrenched from a wife and child in Africa. They promised to try to track him down and convince him to return to the plantation so that, at the very least, he and Victoria could talk and properly say goodbye.

Their search for Barnard was unsuccessful, but in the process they learned the truth about him, after which Victoria no longer wanted to see him or ever hear his name again. The sad story he'd told her, which had softened her heart to him in the first place, had been a lie. He had never been closer to Africa than the east coast of Florida, where he'd been born, and Victoria was not the first indentured servant he'd pursued for her money, with which he would have quickly disappeared after convincing her to run away with him.

Not a day went by, for the rest of Victoria's long, happy life with her new family, that she didn't thank God that she'd stayed where she belonged and let her integrity guide her decisions. She eventually became the nanny to Charlotte's children and died of pneumonia at the age of eighty-six, at great peace with her Father and looking forward to being in His arms again.

JOHN BELUSHI

Comedian, actor, and musician John Belushi completed his fourteenth incarnation in 1982, and he isn't planning to return for another lifetime. There are some spirits who, with the best intentions, eagerly decide to reincarnate, writing charts filled with temptations they know will be very difficult to avoid, and return Home more discouraged than enlightened. Sooner or later they get the message that their lives on the Other Side are simply more productive and worthwhile than their lives on earth could ever be. John is one of those spirits. Excess has repeatedly been a challenge for him here. He's also repeatedly been blessed with an abundance of talent, which made him a born performer in his final lifetime.

John was called Basa in ancient Egypt. He was a performer in some of the earliest satires and a popular harpist at parties thrown by the very wealthy. He was also addicted to opium from the time he was an infant—it was customary for mothers to give opium to their babies to keep them quiet and help them sleep, and opium addiction was perfectly common and not considered to be any danger at all to its user's physical or mental health.

Basa's life was a happy, uneventful one. He was taught by his father to be a skilled carpenter, a trade that would provide him with a comfortable income when he wasn't focused on his great love of performing. He and his mother, a homemaker and occasional singer in the king's court, were especially close. When he was sixteen, he entered into an arranged marriage, fathered three sons, then died at the age of forty-eight of a ruptured colon.

In late eighteenth-century Russia, John's name was Sasha. While his scholastic performance was poor due to dyslexia, his extraordinary athletic ability and coordination led him to a successful career as a dancer in the St. Petersburg ballet. His father owned a brewery, and Sasha, like the majority of his friends and fellow performers, was an avid beer drinker, a highly functioning alcoholic who was deeply in love with his wife, his six children, and his life in general. The cirrhosis of the liver that killed him when he was fifty-eight was undiagnosed, and he died without making any connection between his chronic alcohol consumption and his death.

He was back only five years later for a brief incarnation in Italy. He was named Ciro and from early childhood he had a brilliant operatic voice. His father, a symphony violinist, hired a tutor to coach his young prodigy, and Ciro began touring the country with his father, performing at the private salons of the social elite. It was at these salons that Ciro was introduced to fine wines. As beautifully as he sang, there was nothing more entertaining than this young boy after a glass or two of wine, when he would begin improvising and doing uncanny impersonations of some of the great opera stars of the era, both male and female. Word spread quickly among the wealthy: Essentially, for a good time, hire Ciro. Have him sing, then get him drunk.

Among his biggest fans was a couple in Tuscany who hired him repeatedly and on several occasions invited him and his father to spend the night at their country villa after a performance. They owned, bred, and trained magnificent polo ponies. By the time Ciro was twelve, he had fallen in love with horses and the game of polo. With his father's permission, Ciro accepted the couple's invitation to spend a summer at their ranch, working with and learning to train the ponies. It was an idyllic several weeks, during which Ciro expanded his operatic salon performances to include an amazing display of trick riding on the horses he adored, his inherent fearlessness bolstered by a few glasses of wine. He promised himself that someday he would own a secluded place of his own, like this beautiful private ranch, where he could disappear from time to time—not to escape his growing celebrity, which he loved, but simply to recharge his batteries, so to speak, and work on new performance pieces. (That dream would have to wait a few hundred years, when John Belushi finally found that perfect secluded place on the island of Martha's Vineyard.)

When Ciro was twelve years old and entertaining a group of his hosts' friends with a few trick-riding stunts, spurred by several glasses of wine, he decided to try a handstand on horseback for the first time. He immediately slipped, fell, and hit his head on a rock, which fractured his skull and killed him.

Ten more incarnations followed in rapid succession, all of them with similar patterns—great talent, success at virtually anything he tried, a stunningly coordinated body, and a parade of addictions that became deeply ingrained in John Belushi's cell memory. None of his addictions, he felt, had been to his detriment. In fact, as much as he treasured his life on the Other Side, he came to think of earth as a kind of playground, where he was endlessly welcomed and celebrated by a wide variety of people. But when he decided to return in 1949, only a year after his previous incarnation had ended, and wrote a chart filled with his same patterns, the Council expressed deep concern, feeling sure he was coming back too soon. Without enough insight and recuperation, which could only be accomplished at Home, this time around his excesses were bound to catch up with him.

The Council—also known as the Elders, or the Master Teachers—is its own phylum of eighteen highly advanced male and female spirits who essentially act as God's voice on the Other Side. Council members never incarnate, and their sacred titles are appointed for eternity. They preside in a vast white marble room in the Hall of Justice, at a gleaming white marble U-shaped table, and it's to them that we present the rough drafts of our charts for their divine guidance as one of our final steps before leaving Home to come here. They talk us through every detail of the incarnation we've designed for ourselves, asking questions, advocating modifications, pointing out ways we can maximize the value of the lessons we're intent on learning and areas in which we might be setting ourselves up for more pain and darkness than some lessons are worth.

John Belushi, though, was confident that he and his talent and success would be strong enough to overcome any obstacles in his path, especially with his wife, Judy, by his side. She'd been his best friend and constant companion at Home for centuries and was recruited by his Spirit Guide, Khalil, to accompany him on his last earthly lifetime. Sure enough, all those cell memories, from the best to the worst, caught up with him this time around. He was unprepared, as the Council had feared he might be, when he found himself spinning out of control with no idea of how to make it stop.

KURT COBAIN

Kurt Cobain, the very gifted singer-songwriter-musician who committed suicide in 1994 at the age of twenty-seven—and, yes, it really was a suicide—was only on his eighth incarnation when he died, which is why he seemed like such a young soul to those who knew him. To clarify that statement, all souls—each and every one of us—were created at the same moment an eternity ago. (Eternity, after all, doesn't just mean we always will be; it also means we always were.) The people we perceive as old souls have simply incarnated many, many times on earth, while young souls have experienced relatively few incarnations, which makes them seem new to this world. From an earthly perspective, Kurt was new, deeply sensitive, and with such fresh cell memories from his most recent lifetime that he was still extremely vulnerable to their effects.

In the early 1900s Kurt was born in Nebraska to a busy small-town Christian minister and his wife, a homemaker who was very active in local charities and church activities. Kurt's name was Liam. He was a bright, happy boy, an only child but never at a loss for playmates, between the neighborhood children and his school friends. He loved the hymns sung at church every Sunday and enthusiastically sang along with the rest of the congregation from the time he was three years old. He loved drawing pictures of his favorite Bible stories and helping his mother make cookies and cupcakes for the church's monthly bake sales. Liam's father worked long hours every day, officiating at weddings and funerals, counseling parishioners, teaching Bible studies, and even pitching in to lend a hand when a family in his congregation needed a fence mended, a roof repaired, or a barn built. As a result of all the time they spent alone together, Liam and his mother were very close. The happy, energetic pastor, his gracious wife, and their beautiful little boy were, by all appearances, the perfect family. Liam's was the perfect childhood, he thought.

At first, when Liam turned eleven years old, he didn't sense that something was going wrong. His mother was very careful not to let him see her cry, and there were no raised voices between his parents until after Liam was sound asleep. He finally started to feel an occasional odd tension in the air, to notice a sudden silence between his parents, when he heard his father slam the front door sometimes as he left the house instead of just closing it. Liam asked his mother once if something was wrong, but she assured him everything was fine. Because he wanted to, he believed her.

One night, after what had seemed like a perfectly normal day and evening, Liam was startled awake by the sudden, horrible boom of a gunshot coming from his parents' room. He leaped out of bed and ran out into the hallway, just in time to come face to face with a man wearing a mask and a hat and racing toward the front door. Without a word, the man shot Liam in the stomach, then quickly disappeared.

The next thing Liam knew, he woke up in the hospital in excruciating pain with his father standing beside his bed, weeping. The bullet that had torn through his stomach was lodged too close to his spine to be safely removed without risking paralysis. There wasn't much that could be done, except to keep him bandaged, see to it that his wound didn't get infected, and manage his pain as best they could during his indefinite hospital stay.

He wasn't sure he even cared to live anymore after his father managed to tell him through heartbroken tears that his mother was dead, shot by the same intruder who'd shot Liam. His father stayed by Liam's side day and night, feeding him, praying with him, consoling him, and swearing that he'd never forgive himself for not being home to protect his wife and child.

Liam was weak and in pain and his memory spotty when the police questioned him a week later while his father was out of the room, but he did his best to answer what few questions he could. He couldn't understand why they kept asking him if he was sure that the man with the mask wasn't his father. It devastated him that they could even think such a thing. The police finally explained that, while his father had repeatedly denied having anything to do with it, he'd also failed to provide a verifiable alibi for the night of the murder.

Liam's father was very upset that his young son had been questioned without his being there and that they had been insensitive enough to imply that he might have been involved. The two of them cried together, and that night, with his father holding his hand, Liam passed away, his heart giving out from the severe stomach wound, the stress, and more pain medication than his young body could handle.

He died without knowing the truth: his father was reluctant to divulge his alibi because he'd been with the church secretary that night, with whom he'd been having an affair. Liam's mother had suspected the affair. The secretary's husband, on the other hand, who'd trusted Liam's father and had considered him a friend, had caught the two of them in an inexcusably compromising position. Feeling doubly betrayed by his wife and his pastor, he had decided that since his pastor was taking away his wife, he would take away the pastor's wife in return. He hadn't planned to shoot Liam as well but had impulsively pulled the trigger when Liam had startled him in the hallway. He was eventually convicted of two counts of first-degree murder and given the death penalty, but he died in prison before his execution date.

The impact of cell memory from that incarnation on the life of Kurt Cobain was obvious and immeasurable. That he became angry and withdrawn over his parents' divorce when he was seven is understandable, considering the results of his seemingly happy family in Nebraska being torn apart, though he didn't learn the whole story until he was at Home again and reunited with his beloved mother. And the chronic, excruciating stomach pain he endured for much of his brief lifetime, which had mystified one doctor after another, was actually caused by a gunshot wound more than half a century earlier, when he became the innocent victim of a parent's hypocrisy. It's entirely probable that in his most recent lifetime the nonviolent religions of Buddhism and Jainism, to which Kurt Cobain adhered, were more appealing to him than Christianity after he'd witnessed the behavior of his minister father and a couple of purportedly devout parishioners.

I do want to stress that Kurt Cobain's suicide in no way prevented him from going Home when this incarnation ended. God would never punish suicides resulting from mental impairment, hopelessness, despair, or other circumstances over which a victim has no control. Kurt Cobain is in a blissful state of peace on the Other Side, planning his next incarnation, in which he'll be born in China in February of 2016.

MARTIN LUTHER KING JR.

Dr. King chose to spend eight lifetimes on earth toward the perfection of his spirit, and his most recent and famous one, the one that ended with his assassination in 1968, was his last. But without a doubt the incarnation that most directly impacted the man we knew as one of the greatest leaders of his time began in the early 1700s in Massachusetts.

His name was Thomas, and he had a fraternal twin brother named Andrew. They were the sons of a hellfire-and-brimstone traveling minister named Pastor Byrd. Pastor Byrd preached about a vengeful God and called himself an apostle, ordered by God to mete out judgment and punishment as he saw fit. In reality, this was just the minister's way of controlling everyone around him through fear and giving himself permission to be as cruel and violent as he wanted—a sociopath, in other words, who used God and the Bible to attract and then exploit followers, no more truly righteous or God-centered than Jim Jones or David Koresh. Pastor Byrd's wife was a meek, frightened, insecure woman who obeyed her husband without question and, most horribly, let him discipline Thomas and Andrew with rage and abuse from the time they were babies.

Thomas and Andrew were six years old when one of Pastor Byrd's beatings went too far and Andrew died from his injuries. Thomas never forgave himself for not protecting his brother. He never forgave his father for beating his brother to death. He never forgave his mother for not raising a hand to intervene. But most of all he vowed he would never forgive God, who seemed to be his father's great co-conspirator, so cruel a power that He would allow a child as kind and innocent as Andrew to be killed. There seemed to be no consequences for Pastor Byrd as he pretended to grieve for his beloved son Andrew while describing to anyone who'd listen the tragic fall that had taken his life.

Thomas became understandably detached and introverted, going through the motions of obedience while focusing all his attention on his education. He was extraordinarily bright and left home at age fifteen to pursue a career in medicine. He never saw his parents again and never wanted to. By the time he was twenty, he'd become a successful family doctor, tirelessly traveling on horseback from one patient to another, appreciating a career that kept him too busy to think about the unhealed emotional wounds, the unresolved anger, and the legacy of agnosticism that made him feel separate from everyone around him, even from his own hollow life. That he was living a godly life, kind and compassionate and devoted to healing, never entered his mind. He was simply being true to what he felt was right, as far as he was concerned, and God had nothing to do with it.

One night Thomas was riding through a violent rainstorm when a clap of thunder spooked his horse. Thomas was thrown, and his head hit a rock when he fell, hard enough that he had a classic near-death experience. He traveled through the tunnel, with the impossibly sacred white light of the Holy Spirit at its end. He saw angels. He saw his brother Andrew, happy, thriving, and loving him but telling him that it wasn't time yet, that he had more work to do on earth before he could come Home.

From the moment Thomas opened his eyes again that night, he was a new man—fearless, devoutly spiritual, more dedicated than ever to his medical profession, and an avid student of the Bible, in which he found an unconditionally loving, forgiving God who bore no resemblance to the scary, judgmental, mean-spirited God his father had preached about and used as an excuse to be vicious. Thomas began carrying a Bible with him everywhere he went and sharing the word of God with the families he tended to and stayed with. They shared their faith just as generously with him as well. So, for the first time in his life, Thomas found himself truly connecting, truly belonging, and truly feeling his soul come alive.

When he was in his late forties, Thomas met a young woman who'd been hired as a caretaker for one of his terminally ill patients. She was kind, skilled, and knowledgeable about medicine, and she taught Bible studies at a church near the patient's home. Thomas began attending her Bible classes and working side by side with her for his patient's comfort. His admiration for her was only exceeded by his attraction to her. The feelings were mutual, and they quickly developed a serious, deeply loving relationship. Tragically, two weeks before they had planned to marry, Thomas died suddenly of a heart attack.

He arrived Home with a great sense of peace about the lifetime he'd just completed. During it, he'd developed a cherished, ironclad relationship with God, he'd become fearless in the face of cruelty, he'd learned the joy of honoring God by devoting his life to serving His children, and he'd found love with a remarkable woman.

It was that spirit, with those lessons fully intact, who was eager to come back to earth for one more incarnation, as the historic presence we knew as Martin Luther King Jr., and with that same remarkable woman we knew as Coretta Scott King by his side again so that they could finish their journeys together.

GILDA RADNER

The gifted, utterly captivating actress and comedienne Gilda Radner, whose brave, public battle against ovarian cancer is still inspiring countless cancer patients today, left her thirty-first incarnation behind in 1989 and will be back to this world three more times. She feels she has much more work to do to fully satisfy her recurring life theme of catalyst.

As its name suggests, those with a catalyst theme are the movers and shakers of the world. They make things happen, they take action when something needs to be done, and they're incapable of sitting idly by if they believe they can have a positive influence on a situation, whether or not they had anything to do with creating that situation in the first place.

She's also an example of some truly dramatic effects of cell memory in action, most of them from an incarnation in a small town in Texas in the late 1800s. Her name was Mandy, and she was the only child of an oil worker and his high-maintenance wife, Jane. She adored her father and did her best to adore and understand her mother, who Mandy recognized very early in her life was someone who created drama out of nothing and everything, if only to keep herself stimulated. Her mother was also prone to wild mood swings, from euphoric to anxious, and depressed with no apparent explanation.

The histrionics severely escalated when Jane became pregnant with Mandy's little brother. Mandy was eight years old when her brother was born two months premature and eight years old when her father suddenly disappeared during Jane's pregnancy and was never seen again. "He ran off with another woman" was the only explanation Jane offered. Mandy pretended to believe her but, in her heart of hearts, never could imagine that her father would have left her without saying goodbye.

Between her baby's fragile medical condition, her husband's disappearance, and the fact that there was suddenly no money coming in, Jane insisted that Mandy quit school and take care of her brother while Jane found what work she could cleaning houses. This created a very strong bond between Mandy and baby Dale. She was as relieved as her mother was when his doctors announced on his third birthday that, while he would always be small and his immune system compromised, he had finally turned a corner and was going to be okay, as long as they were careful to keep him strong and well nourished. This inspired a running mealtime comment from Jane, presumably as a reminder that, despite Jane's hard work at a job she loathed and resented, they had very little money: "Don't forget, Mandy. The more you eat, the less there is for your brother."

Mandy never forgot. She developed severe eating disorders as a result of feeling guilty with every bite she took, and those same disorders, thanks to cell memory, continued to plague her in her next incarnation as Gilda Radner.

Despite not being in school, Mandy's innate intelligence and her aspirations compelled her to keep studying the one subject that she loved. She was determined to become a great writer someday, in pursuit of which she had become a voracious reader, fascinated to figure out why some books were easy to set aside while others were so compelling she couldn't put them down until she'd finished them. She'd begun writing wonderful short stories when she was seven years old. She also wrote her observations and private thoughts in a journal every night before she fell asleep, which she kept hidden under her mattress. It was a habit she'd learned from her mother.

From time to time she wondered where Jane hid her own journal. She would occasionally search for it while her mother was at work, especially when she was missing her father and wondering how another woman could have appeared so suddenly in his life and become more important to him than his own family.

When Mandy was thirteen, she began menstruating, with extremely painful cramps and irritability. The family doctor prescribed for her what he'd prescribed for Jane years earlier and, in the process, solved the mystery of Jane's wild mood swings: morphine. Jane had taken the drug for the duration of each menstrual cycle and had become addicted. Mandy, while she appreciated the relief from her pain and moodiness, thanks to the injections that Jane routinely and expertly gave her every few weeks, hated the feeling of not being in control of her own mind. With the thought of becoming as unpredictable as her mother, Mandy managed through sheer force of will to limit her morphine use to those few injections per month.

One day, on yet another search for Jane's journals, Mandy discovered some loose floorboards in the back of her mother's closet. She lifted them and found a library of thick, worn leather journals. Her heart was pounding as she picked out the journal and the pages pertaining to the dates of her father's disappearance, and it stopped when she read the real story.

Jane, with an eight-year-old daughter to raise and pregnant with her son, had gone to the vast field behind their house, where her husband was repairing a fence, in order to confront him about the family finances and demand for the hundredth time that he get a second job. He, for the hundredth time, had pointed out that he was too exhausted and well paid enough from the job he already had and that they would be fine, if Jane would learn to control her spending habits. The argument had escalated into a shoving match, culminating in a strong push from her that had caused him to lose his balance and fall into a deep abandoned well. She had stood there in shock for quite some time, listening for a cry for help or even a groan of pain, but she'd heard nothing at all. Correctly assuming that the fall had killed him, Jane had simply taken the long walk back to the house and, on the way, concocted the story she'd told Mandy about her father abandoning them for someone else.

Mandy was both relieved and horrified to learn the truth and feel the betrayal of her mother's massive lie. She wrote a long, eloquent letter, detailing everything she'd discovered and, with her beloved little brother Dale, walked two miles to their nearest neighbor and left the letter and the journal on their doorstep. She then did her best to act as if nothing had happened when her mother came home.

That night, Jane heard Mandy sobbing in her room and went to check on her, morphine syringe in hand. Mandy accepted the injection as always, not noticing that it took a bit longer than usual to empty the syringe into her arm.

Jane's last words to her daughter were "One of my journals is missing. I know that's why you're crying, and I'm sorry, but I have to make sure you'll never tell anyone."

Mandy was dead by morning of a morphine overdose.

Jane, by the way, thanks to the efforts of both Mandy and the concerned neighbor, was eventually convicted of the involuntary death of her husband and the murder of her daughter. Six-year-old Dale was adopted by that same neighbor, raised with love and compassion, and went on to become a Texas Ranger.

In her latest life, ill with ovarian cancer, Gilda Radner entered the hospital. She became resistant to being sedated because she was sure she would never wake up again. Gilda was unconscious when she returned to her room from the CAT scan, and she went Home three days later without ever regaining consciousness.

MARLON BRANDO

On-screen and off, legendary actor and activist against racial prejudice Marlon Brando was one of a kind. *TIME* magazine even named him one of its One Hundred Persons of the Century in a 1999 retrospective issue. The incarnation Brando completed on July 1, 2004, was his twenty-seventh, and he intends to live four more lifetimes on earth before he considers this part of his soul's journey complete.

From the moment he first set foot on the island of Tahiti when filming *Mutiny on the Bounty*, Brando felt a deep connection, a stirring of his cell memory that's a perfect example of the phenomenon called morphic resonance. Morphic resonance happens when the spirit mind finds itself in a place so profoundly familiar from a past life that it experiences almost total recall and infuses the conscious mind with that same, seemingly inexplicable sense of familiarity. In Brando's case, that morphic resonance dated all the way back to the eighth century. So during his 1960 trip to Tahiti he legitimately felt that he was coming home.

His name had been Fara, and he was a Tahitian clan noble with a title that was ancestrally inherited rather than earned. He was privileged and spoiled from birth by a mother who had a pathological mistrust of females. She had never particularly cared for her five daughters so was ecstatic at the arrival of her only son, especially knowing he would grow up to be a member of the clan's elite. She never said no to him; nor did she allow his older sisters to refuse him anything or disagree with him. On the rare occasions when he was denied something he wanted, Fara quickly learned that a combination of his hair-trigger temper and a long, loud tantrum would turn things around.

By the time Fara was in his late teens and of an age to be enthroned, his typically absent father had properly prepared him for the responsibilities of his position as a noble. He'd also learned and taken to heart the cultural belief that clan nobles were descendants of the gods. When he was formally presented with the belt of red feathers that proclaimed his elevated status in the clan, he embraced it as permission to act out his sense of entitlement and indulge in his deep commitment to hedonism.

He promptly took six wives in addition to many mistresses, resulting in a total of twenty-seven children, all of whom knew to expect nothing from him beyond an occasional audience and his expectation of their slavish obedience to his arbitrary, often eccentric rules; otherwise, they would face the full force of his considerable temper. Meals were to be served to him every three hours, for example, whether he wanted them or not (although he usually did, and he took great pride in his obesity, seeing it as a sign of success). And his feet were to be washed six times a day, one of the countless signs of his acquired germ phobia. Although there had been no threats against him, and he surrounded himself with guards twenty-four hours a day, he employed a servant whose only responsibility was to taste Fara's food and drink in his presence, before Fara ate his meals, to confirm that no one was trying to poison him.

And because it was believed that clan nobles possessed supernatural powers as part of their divine lineage, Fara created fabulous legends about nonexistent enemy ships he'd made disappear before they'd reached the island, victorious wrestling matches with demons who were trying to destroy the clan chief (matches that always took place in the privacy of his quarters and when no one else was around), and his uncanny ability to make the sands of the beaches softer to the touch with a wave of his hand (and of course no one dared point out that the sand felt about the same as it had before he'd waved his hand). Fara also delighted in crediting his powers with the most ordinary natural events—when it rained, when it stopped raining, when the tide came in, when the tide went out, when a citrus crop was prolific, when a citrus crop failed, when a shooting star was spotted in the night sky, when the moon changed phases. All of it happened, he loved to say, because his powers willed it to be so. Not once did it occur to him that there might be some eye-rolling occurring behind his back at these claims.

Perhaps one of the most remarkable aspects of Fara's life was that for all his hedonistic excess and pretense, he loved every minute of it. He was living in what he was sure was the most beautiful place in the universe. He was refused nothing. He had all that he wanted of everything he wanted. Very little was expected of him. And when obesity-related diabetes ended that incarnation on his fifty-first birthday, he closed his eyes for the last time with no regrets whatsoever. Depth, sensitivity, tears, and spirituality would come later.

A brief lifetime as a brave in the Salish tribe in the Pacific Northwest during the 1800s left another indelible mark on Brando's soul. His name, as best I can understand it from Spirit Guide Francine's rapid, high-pitched chirping, sounds something like Hataya, and no one ever felt more deeply or believed more passionately in the sanctity of nature. Hataya treasured the thick forests that surrounded his village and could survive alone in them for weeks at a time in search of valuable pelts. Every tree and plant was a rich source of food and oils that could heal wounds. Every broken branch and disturbed pile of leaves told a story of recent movement. Each breeze carried valuable scents, and the silence of dark nights allowed him to eavesdrop on whatever secrets the land and its creatures cared to whisper. Every day he was grateful for his finely tuned instincts and humbled to be living in such a sacred place.

At every new moon Hataya returned to his tribe's village with pelts and food. While he held his family and the elders in the highest respect, he only stayed for a few short hours at a time, becoming overwhelmed and claustrophobic in the company of so many people, and soon stole back into the thick trees where he felt peace.

The arrival of the white man—the fur traders and trappers, and the missionaries eager to bring the word of Christ—was generally welcomed by the Native Americans in the area. Hataya, on the other hand, was quietly appalled at the disregard with which they treated his beloved land, especially the noisy hunting parties who trampled and littered his forest. He never spoke to them. He instead avoided them, more heart-broken than angry. During one of these intrusions, after he realized they weren't going away, he went to his cherished mother and knelt before her, weeping. "I can't hear the earth anymore," he said

She didn't try to stop him when he disappeared into the woods again. He went to a hidden inlet of the once-clear stream, lay down, and covered himself with leaves and rocks. At the age of twenty-one he died of exposure, or as his mother and the other tribal elders believed, he willed himself to die. He was free of his body within days and, on returning Home, promised himself and God that he would never again stand by silently while the earth or any of its inhabitants were defiled. And the greater the voice he was given, the more loudly he would speak out.

In one of the four remaining lifetimes he'll spend here, he'll speak out even more loudly than he did as Marlon Brando, when he becomes a U.S. president with an unprecedented passion for the environment and racial equality.

HUMPHREY BOGART

Called "the greatest male star in the history of American cinema" by the American Film Institute, Humphrey Bogart brought to his final incarnation the accumulated wisdom and experience of forty-six previous lifetimes. That he wasn't a performer in any of his past lives is a little surprising, considering his legendary acting skills, but other aspects of his life—his love of the sea, his lifelong passion for chess, his attraction to strong women, his general habit of success, even his disdain for pretense and phoniness—are traceable to his soul's rich history.

He was born in Norway in the late tenth century to a hardworking logger and his wife, a tiny tough-as-nails homemaker. He was named Falcor, and although he was short in stature, he was uncommonly strong, a tireless worker, and utterly fearless—the first to jump in when there was a potentially dangerous job to be done. It was assumed that Falcor would follow in his father's footsteps into the logging business, but when he was twelve years old his uncle, whom he idolized, came to visit and enchanted him with stories of his life as a merchant seaman. With his parents' approval, Falcor went to live with his uncle for a year on the North Atlantic coast. He fell in love with the sea and became a remarkably skilled sailor. He told his parents that he never felt closer to God than when he was watching the sun sinking into the endless water when a day's work was through.

He met his wife, Nessa, when they were both eighteen. She was a stoneworker at her father's quarry and reminded him of his mother—tough and tender, tireless, without a word of complaint, and perfectly capable of taking care of herself. If she were going to have a man in her life, he would have to earn the right to be her partner, not her boss. Falcor loved and admired her and was proud to be married to her.

It was through Nessa, in fact, and her family connections that he found himself on the great adventure of his life—Falcor was a member of the Viking crew that sailed from Norway with Leif Ericson when Ericson discovered a place he called Vinland on the northern tip of what's now Newfoundland. Even at its most brutal, the journey thrilled Falcor, and he vowed to return to settle there with Nessa someday.

Leif Ericson had converted Falcor, along with several other crewmembers, to Christianity en route to North America and recruited Falcor and his family to be part of a mission to introduce Christianity to Greenland. Falcor, Nessa, and Falcor's parents willingly relocated. Falcor and his father were instrumental in starting a lumber mill there, and Nessa and Falcor were ecstatic at the arrival of two healthy baby boys.

Eight years after they arrived in Greenland, Falcor, Nessa, and their sons left for Vinland and took up residence in one of the Norse settlements there. It was an idyllic life for Falcor in particular, a perfect combination of wilderness and the sea, and the family might have stayed forever if Nessa hadn't developed a lingering illness that required more expert medical attention than the settlement could provide. They headed back to Greenland, where Nessa died six months later of what we would now call lymphoma. By now Falcor's father's health was beginning to fail as well, and without resentment or regret, Falcor gave up his travels at sea in order to work at his father's lumber mill, side by side with his sons.

Sadly, Falcor died before his father. He was alone in the forest cutting trees when a fluke accident with his ax severed an artery, and he bled to death before he could get to help. He went to the Other Side a deeply satisfied, peaceful man, having lived every minute of the life he'd chosen.

Bogart's connection to the game of chess was even more direct than his passion for sailing. In sixteenth-century Portugal, his name was Luis. He had an older brother and sister, and their mother had died giving birth to him. Their father was bedridden with cerebral palsy by the time Luis was twelve, which made it necessary for the children to work in order to care for him. They found what odd jobs they could, staggering their hours so that their father would never be left alone, and when they were at home, they took turns entertaining their father by playing chess with him, a game he loved, which was gaining popularity throughout Europe.

An idea evolved between Luis and his siblings that they might be able to make a far better living and work from home by applying their artistic talents to making hand-carved chess pieces and creating inlaid chess-boards. The older brother was the perfect answer to promoting the new business—while he lacked the art-istry it took to execute the chess sets themselves, he'd gained a reputation throughout the area as a master chess player and had become a popular guest at chess parties thrown by those who were determined to beat him. By insisting on bringing one of the beautiful chess sets Luis and their sister had created for all his matches, he attracted a constant parade of customers to the modest but prolific in-home studio. That they were now able to take great care of their father and that he admired their work, gave them enormous plea-sure. And while it frustrated Luis a bit that he was only rarely able to beat his brother at the game, for the most part he was very proud of him and enjoyed promoting his career as a master chess player every bit as much as his brother enjoyed promoting the shop.

It might also have been during these years that Bogart's disdain for phoniness began. Luis was incred-ulous that their wealthiest customers were invariably the most demanding and the slowest to pay, or the most likely to try to avoid paying at all. "We have very influential friends," they would say, "and you'll make far more than what we owe you by simply letting us show off your work to them." Another favorite was, "Rather than giving you money, we've brought you two bottles of wine from our vineyards whose value far exceeds what we owe you." Luis had no trouble saying no to these people and was fascinated at how frequently his saying no only made them more determined to shop at his family's thriving little studio.

Luis's wife in that lifetime was the home health-care worker they hired for their father when his needs exceeded their knowledge and ability. She was compassionate but firm, honest, skilled, and loved her work. She had a surprising, refreshing sense of humor, and she even insisted on learning to play chess, because it helped keep their father's mind stimulated. It attracted Luis even more that he had to ask her three times to marry him before she finally accepted. She was unable to have children and wanted to be sure that he meant it when he had said having children wasn't important to him. They lived a long, happy life together. Luis died of lung disease at the remarkably old age of eighty-six and his wife died exactly one week later on her eighty-second birthday. It's interesting that no one from this or any of Bogart's other past lives reappeared in his final incarnation.

AMELIA EARHART

Undoubtedly the world's most famous aviatrix and the subject of one of aviation's most legendary unsolved mysteries, Amelia Earhart's fifty-second and final incarnation was the culmination of lives lived challenging boundaries and refusing to accept socially prescribed limits. Fifteen of those lives were spent as a male, which makes it perfectly understandable that Amelia found it impossible to process the idea that certain doors would be closed to her for no other reason than her gender. If she'd had conscious recall of her past lives, she might easily have said, "I've been a Roman gladiator, a Turkish warrior, a decorated member of the Royal Navy, and a Norwegian explorer. And you're going to tell me I'm not qualified to vote because I happen to be inhabiting a woman's body this time around?"

The incarnation immediately preceding the one for which she was best known was spent as a male and typified her fearlessness, her independence, and her innate belief in the sheer logic of equal rights on behalf of men as well as women. In the early 1800s, Amelia was a boy named John, the third child born to a horse rancher in what is now Texas. John's father was a fun and devoted dad, the prototypical man's man, who could rope, ride, sharp-shoot, build a fence or a barn or a house from the ground up, hold his liquor, and play a good game of poker. John's mother was as feminine as his father was masculine. She was a tiny, pretty woman, who loved her two daughters and her son almost as much as she hated life on the "godforsaken ranch" for which she'd left her parents' lovely home in civilized Virginia. She was an excellent mother, homemaker, and Christian. Every night she read the Bible to her children instead of bedtime stories. But her hatred of the family's lifestyle, so far from home and miles from the closest neighbor, inevitably compromised her feelings for her husband. She slowly sank into a depression, which made it more and more difficult for her to function normally.

Finally John's parents made the difficult decision that she and their children would be better off and the children would receive a better education, if they moved back to her wealthy parents' home in Virginia and left John's father on the ranch where he was so happy and financially invested. John was eight years old and unbearably sad to leave his father and a life he loved. As young as he was, he was also outraged that his mother was being allowed to keep the children just because she was their mother while their father, a very loving, hands-on father, seemed to have no say in the matter at all. But John went to Virginia with his mother and sisters, without complaint, while quietly planning his escape.

For four years he worked hard doing odd jobs for his grandparents and their neighbors, grateful for any pocket change they were willing to pay and equally grateful that his mother never thought to ask what he was doing with that pocket change. Then one night, when he was twelve years old, he gathered every penny he'd earned, packed a small satchel, left a note for his family, telling them where he was going and not to worry, and excitedly made his way back to his father's ranch by stagecoach or any other means he could find.

It's an understatement to say that his father was surprised and ecstatic to see him, especially after he'd been reassured that John hadn't left a frantic family back in Virginia not knowing where he'd gone. Father and son resumed their lives together. John industriously worked around the ranch, side by side with his father, and became his father's talented, enthusiastic, and utterly fearless student. There was nothing he wouldn't try and persevere at until he excelled. By his late teens John could out-ride, out-rope, and out-shoot his father, and more often than not beat him at poker at the nearby saloon. John also became one of the best trick riders anyone had ever seen and made good prize money at competitions throughout the area. He was the first to put up signs on every fence post and saloon wall to publicize his upcoming appearances, and he became somewhat of a local celebrity. When he was twenty-two he married one of his most loyal admirers, the daughter of a cattle rancher who traveled many miles to attend his events and made no secret of her attraction to him. Together John and his father built a house for the happy newlyweds on the family ranch, and the three of them thrived on their closeness and mutual love of the simple, hard-working, hard-playing life they shared.

When Texas was called upon to provide soldiers for the Confederate army, it was in perfect keeping with John's unhesitating, adventurous courage that he was among the first to enlist. His wife and father sadly but proudly waved goodbye to him, knowing he'd likely place himself on the front line of any battle with no thought of the harm that might come to him.

John was indeed on the front line of the Galveston battle in 1863 and was one of the few Confederate soldiers to die there. He went Home peacefully, with a deep sense of satisfaction for a lifetime he'd truly lived and insisted on enjoying without letting fear get in his way. He left behind a father and wife he loved and knew would take care of each other.

It's very unusual for a spirit to reincarnate within just a few decades. But it was well known on the Other Side—thanks in great part to the constant research and design work that occurs there and is sent to this world through infused knowledge—that a thrilling new invention called a flying machine was about to be unveiled on earth, and John wasn't about to miss out on experiencing and mastering it. That it would be an even more extraordinary accomplishment for a woman than for a man seemed laughably apparent.

And so it was that Amelia Earhart insisted on being born in 1897. In the context of her soul's eternal journey, she achieved every goal she charted for herself, including leaving an indelible mark on the history of aviation, as the mystery of her disappearance continues.

JAMES STEWART

The wonderful, unassuming actor, war veteran, and family man we knew as Jimmy Stewart completed his fifty-first and final incarnation on July 2, 1997, with past lives that most certainly foreshadowed his most celebrated time on earth.

In the mid-1700s he was born to a lighthouse keeper and his wife on an island off the New England coast. His name was Ethan, and he was an uncommonly small child, quiet and sensitive, who loved reading, gardening and baking wonderful desserts with his mother for the two of them to sell on the mainland. He very much admired his father's work ethic and accepted without question or complaint the fact that his father was an emotionally distant, unaffectionate man who was almost pathologically reclusive. Ethan was seventeen when his parents died in a boating accident during a violent storm. His grief over losing them never quite subsided and made him even more introverted, and he was utterly content to stay on the island and assume the responsibilities and lodging of the lighthouse.

Ethan was twenty and picking up supplies on the mainland when he met a woman named Mary, twelve years his senior, who had begun working in the local dry goods store when her husband passed away. Mary was lovely, soft-spoken, and creative, and the two of them immediately recognized each other as kindred spirits. They married and set up housekeeping in the island lighthouse. Mary's paintings of the lighthouse, the passing ships, and the occasionally angry skies over the ocean were greatly admired and sold to enthusiastic buyers on the mainland, and Ethan and Mary spent some of the proceeds to have her beloved piano shipped to the island from her former home in Delaware. She taught Ethan to play, giving him an outlet for his life-long love of music, and he taught her to bake and to garden. They loved taking long walks together and reading great literature to each other by the fire on cold North Atlantic nights, and just when they thought the quiet, happy life they'd created couldn't be more perfect, they joyfully discovered that Mary was pregnant.

That joy vanished when Mary died giving birth to their son, William. Ethan treasured the little boy as Mary's legacy and raised him well, and for many years he and William were inseparable. William inherited his mother's artistic talents and his parents' love of music. Sadly, he was also prone to deep depressions, blaming himself for his mother's death and his father's quiet loneliness despite Ethan's best efforts to the contrary, and by the time he was in his late teens William had become intensely withdrawn. He would create dark, disquieting pencil sketches and spend intense hours at a time at the piano without speaking. He developed insomnia and a loss of appetite that would last for days on end. Ethan, desperate to rescue his son from his escalating emotional turmoil, sought help for William on the mainland. But the stress of loving and living with a young man for whom he'd been solely

responsible but couldn't seem to comfort took a devastating toll on Ethan—he died of heart disease at the
age of forty-two. A few short hours later, William took
his own life, swimming far out into the Atlantic and
drowning himself in the sea with the lighthouse barely
visible through a thick, cold fog.

Many lifetimes later, William was a friend and fellow
soldier of Jimmy Stewart's in World War II, and Mary
married Ethan again when she was known as Jimmy's
beloved wife Gloria.

Another of Jimmy Stewart's most significant incarnations was in North Carolina, where he was born in
1840 to a preacher and his very sweet, very devoted
wife. They gave him the biblically inspired name Joseph,
never nicknamed Joe, and they adored him. In addition
to his heavy Southern drawl, Joseph was born with a
stutter that made him self-conscious as a young child.

An unexpected transformation presented itself in the
form of an elderly black man named Charles, caretaker
of the house next door to the parsonage where Joseph
and his parents lived. Charles ended each day sitting on
the front porch of the house singing gospel songs and
accompanying himself on the banjo. Joseph was drawn
to the music and to Charles, who was a kind, empathetic man, and Charles was happy to teach Joseph not
only how to play the banjo but also how to harmonize

on those wonderful spiritual songs. Incredibly, the two of them discovered that Joseph didn't stutter in the slightest when he sang.

There was nothing remarkable about Joseph's singing voice, but it gave him confidence, and he embraced singing as his primary form of communication. He also loved to write short stories about a little boy who, after his parents were asleep, would travel on a magical boat that could fly to faraway places—by no coincidence, places in which Joseph had spent some of his past lives, including a small island off the coast of New England where the boy created a beautiful garden. Children who had once teased Joseph about his stuttering now gravitated to him, eager to hear him sing his wonderful stories while accompanying himself on the banjo. He came to equate performing with self-confidence and success, and his proud, supportive parents encouraged him by arranging for banjo lessons and tutoring sessions in creative writing with a church member who wrote for the local newspaper.

Joseph fought proudly and courageously in the Civil War, then married his childhood sweetheart, a smart, happy girl named Beth who loved to cook. They set up housekeeping a short distance from Joseph's parents, attended church every Sunday, and raised eight children, supporting their family by opening a small neighborhood restaurant featuring Beth's homespun cooking and Joseph's desserts—he'd learned to bake and showed an "odd" affinity for it. It was a popular feature of the restaurant that, on request, Joseph would sing the menu rather than present the printed version. He also became a contributing writer for the local newspaper.

Joseph was seventy-three when he died of an aneurism. Beth passed away from pneumonia only two months later. They were reunited in their most recent lives when Beth returned as Jimmy Stewart's daughter Kelly.

Jimmy Stewart brought many facets of his past lives with him into his last incarnations, from his love of gardening, to his offstage interest in playing a musical instrument, to the comfort he found in performing, to the sense of duty that compelled him to be a soldier, to his tendency toward being an introvert, to his hobby of writing, to the slight shadow of a stutter, to the cell memory of death from a circulatory disorder.

GIANNI VERSACE

Few designers come as naturally to their artistic brilliance as the late Gianni Versace, whose forty-first and final incarnation ended suddenly and tragically when he was only fifty. He'd been a celebrated designer in a past life in France as well, perhaps the most influential of his previous incarnations for a variety of reasons.

His name then was Etienne. He was born in Paris in the mid-1600s to a successful tailor and his seamstress wife, who specialized in creating men's and women's formal wear and were known for working with only the finest, most exclusive fabrics. Etienne, the youngest of six children, was the only one who showed both an interest in and an extraordinary talent for his parents' trade. While his brothers and sisters were busily pursuing their love of everything from astronomy to architecture to theology (two of his brothers ultimately entered the priesthood), Etienne could be found with a sketchpad, drawing unique fashion designs and, with his parents' encouragement, recreating them on dress forms in their shop. Some of his gowns were too innovative for their clients' tastes, but with more experience and an uncanny instinct for styles that would be gaining popularity in the near future, he created a following of his own that he loyally shared with his parents, remaining in their shop with them long past a time when he could so easily have gone out on his own. He became the shop's sole proprietor when his parents retired.

Etienne literally married the girl next door at age sixteen, and he and his fifteen-year-old bride expressed their adoration of children by having eleven of them, including two sets of twins, by the time they were in their mid-twenties. The hard work and expense of raising such a large family were a challenge; Etienne was at his shop for long hours seven days a week to keep up. His only regret was that there weren't enough hours in the day to do more for his beloved wife and children.

So when a courier arrived at his shop one day, summoning him to an audience at Versailles with an aide to King Louis XIV, Etienne couldn't have been more shocked and intrigued. It seemed the king had been monitoring the private letters of the resident designer, Henri, who provided wardrobes for the king's mistresses, and he had found that the designer was complaining about the king behind his back, making unflattering comments, and passing along gossip that should never have left the palace walls. Etienne's excellent reputation had reached Versailles, so the king wanted him to replace Henri as the mistresses' exclusive designer. He would be very handsomely paid, and because the king was aware of Etienne's large family, Etienne would be allowed two days a week at home while living the other five in his well-appointed quarters in the palace.

It was a once-in-a-lifetime opportunity, Etienne and his wife agreed, much too generous to pass up.

His retired parents moved into the house to help with the children, and Etienne moved into his small apartment in the Versailles compound. Eerily, when he first arrived, he found an angry, menacing-looking man in his late thirties staring in at him through the open apartment door as Etienne began to unpack. "You've taken what was mine and destroyed my life, and I will destroy yours," the man said before being escorted to the gates by a palace guard. Etienne discovered that it had been Henri, and although he was shaken, he was soon too involved in his work and his new surroundings to be preoccupied by a threat from a clearly unstable man.

His privileged existence at Versailles and the satisfaction of beautifully dressing the king's mistresses were appealing but didn't prevent Etienne from desperately missing his family. He made the most of his two days a week with them, and his generous pay made it possible for him to buy a spacious house for his wife, children, and parents on the outskirts of Paris, much closer to his part-time residence, as well as to hire a governess to help care for and educate his children. His talent and loyalty inspired favor with the king; within a few years he was also designing wardrobes for the queen's ladies-in-waiting and creating gowns for the queen herself.

Life seemed almost perfect until one night when Etienne was at home with his family. Suddenly, the house burst into flames. Everyone managed to escape before the devastating fire destroyed the house and everything inside, but a torch was found outside a heavily draped open window, clearly indicating arson. The few witnesses who stepped forward described a man they had seen lurking near the house, torch in hand, shortly before the fire had started. The description perfectly matched Henri, about whom Etienne had long since forgotten. It was one thing to threaten Etienne, but to endanger the lives of everyone he loved was unspeakable. Etienne refused to let it happen again.

When the palace guards and the gendarmes were unable to track down Henri, Etienne resigned his position at Versailles, to the king's indignation but with the sympathy of the queen and her court. He then moved his family to a small village in Belgium, and he hired guards to protect them around the clock. He maintained a low profile by doing nothing more than occasional tailoring work in his house. His many precautions seemed to accomplish their purpose. Etienne died of pancreatitis at the age of eighty-four, his wife died of pneumonia on her ninetieth birthday, and all eleven of his children went on to live long, full, successful lives of their own.

Gianni Versace experienced several reunions from his life in the 1600s in his final incarnation. His sister Donatella was his wife in that lifetime. A niece and nephew to whom he was particularly close were two of his beloved children back then. The most tragically memorable reunion, though, occurred in front of his home in Miami, Florida, on July 15, 1997, when he was shot and killed seemingly for no reason by a man named Andrew Cunanan, who hundreds of years ago had been known as Henri.

LANA TURNER

Lana Turner was one of Hollywood's most glamorous and most notorious stars, juggling a busy career with eight marriages, seven husbands, and a widely publicized controversial murder in the family. Her most recent incarnation, her forty-fifth, was certainly her most dramatic, and it won't be her last—she plans to return one more time as a cancer researcher in Denmark, a continuation of her ongoing work on the Other Side, searching for a cure for the throat cancer that killed her in 1995.

The vast majority of her incarnations were varied and fairly unremarkable. She lived several of them in South America—four in Argentina and three in Brazil—and even more of them in the Far East, with a pattern of trying over and over again to find an escape from poverty and into a peaceful security within herself, which continually seemed to elude her. Insecurity plagued her in most of her lifetimes, no matter what she looked like, mostly because she kept turning to those around her to determine an opinion of herself and because she seemed to lose her sense of her God-centeredness every time she left Home, and then couldn't find her way back to it until she returned to the Other Side again.

There's no doubt that her most significant point-of-entry lifetime began in Oklahoma in about 1860. Her name was Mary, and her parents were madly in love sixteen-year-olds who, needless to say, were completely unprepared to share the responsibility of a child or even stay together, as it turned out. Her father's parents packed up their son and left town as quickly as possible, leaving Mary's mother, Laura, to fend for herself with the very little help her own parents had to offer.

Laura turned out to be a loving and devoted mother, for someone so young, and she gratefully accepted whatever jobs she could find cleaning houses. She left Mary with her grandmother during her long hours at work and contributed to the household rent and food expenses. When Mary was four years old, an opportunity came along for a whole new life for her and her mother. Laura's favorite uncle was opening a poker club in Biloxi, Mississippi, and he offered Laura a job as a bartender and singer. Laura and Mary could stay with him and his wife until Laura got on her feet, at which point he would help her find her own place. The pay was acceptable—certainly more than Laura was making as a housekeeper—and she'd been feeling badly about being a grown woman living with her parents and adding a noisy, active baby to the mix. So Laura gratefully accepted the offer and, with her parents' blessing, headed with Mary to the Gulf Coast.

Laura and Mary fell in love with Biloxi, from their almost daily trips to the beach to the smell of the ocean air to the modest but thriving poker club where Laura immediately began working. Laura's aunt and uncle enjoyed their company, and Laura's aunt watched and homeschooled Mary during Laura's long hours at work, an arrangement that continued even after Laura rented a small apartment for herself and her daughter a few blocks away.

The men at the club liked and respected Laura, who'd always been able to hold her own in a room full of males. She was friendly but not flirtatious, and after a couple of years Laura felt comfortable enough with a few of them to let them continue their poker games at her apartment after the club closed for the night, provided they kept the noise down and didn't disturb her sleeping daughter. Mary had become well known at the club, loving to visit her mother at work and bask in all that male attention. Laura's private poker games became a time-honored tradition, and Laura was grateful to supplement her income with the customary generous tips from the players.

Eight years passed fairly unremarkably. Laura continued enjoying her work at the poker club, and the private parties afterwards, and became involved in a couple of serious relationships but ultimately decided she was happier on her own. Mary thrived at school, loved swimming in the ocean and reading, and grew prettier by the minute. The normalcy of their lives made what happened early one morning even more of a shock.

It was 4:00 A.M. That night's group of poker players had left the apartment about an hour earlier. Laura was startled out of a sound sleep by a piercing scream coming from Mary's room. She grabbed the gun she kept under her bed, raced to her daughter's bedroom, threw open the door, and saw a man with a gag in his hands darting away from Mary's bed and escaping out the window. Laura ran to the window and fired a shot into the darkness, but the man was gone.

Mary was terrified but untouched—she'd screamed the instant she'd heard the man climb in through the window. Laura's immediate arrival had undoubtedly saved her from being molested or kidnapped. If possible, Laura was even more traumatized than her daughter. It had been too dark for either of them to see the man's face, which meant it could have been a stranger, someone from the poker club, or even one of the men who'd been in their apartment for a few after-hours hands of five-card stud. The invasion itself was horrible enough, but Laura was haunted by not knowing who had tried to sneak into Mary's room and rape her. She decided to pack up their belongings and move back into her parents' house in Oklahoma, leaving behind a life they'd both loved but grateful for the peace of mind it would bring them.

Mary's teen years hit hard. After a head-spinning variety of boyfriends, at the age of seventeen she ran off to California with a thirty-year-old businessman, despite Laura's efforts to dissuade her. Laura took care of her parents until they passed away, then put herself through school and became a nurse. Mary showed up on her doorstep ten years later, broke and divorced, and with an autistic son. Laura, of course, took them in. The three of them lived together for the rest of their lives. Laura died at the age of sixty-six of congestive heart failure while Mary, who outlived her son, lived to be eighty-three, when a ruptured appendix ended that incarnation.

In a later century and a different lifetime, the fabulous movie star Lana Turner was involved with an abusive aspiring actor and alleged small-time gangster named Johnny Stompanato. She had decided to break up with him, and on Good Friday in 1958 a terrible fight ensued between Lana and Johnny behind her closed bedroom door. Laura—now Lana Turner's fourteen-year-old daughter, Cheryl Crane—heard the fight, ran to the kitchen, and grabbed a knife. After some chaos and confusion, she stabbed and killed Johnny Stompanato. A sensational trial ended with a jury ruling the stabbing a justifiable homicide and acquitting Cheryl Crane. In a way, even though their mother–daughter roles had been reversed in their second incarnation together, Laura (Cheryl) finally succeeded, instinctively and absolutely justifiably, in protecting her daughter Mary (Lana) from a serious threat to her safety.

I admit I was a little surprised, and disappointed, to learn that Johnny Stompanato was not a reincarnation of the man who had slipped into Mary's bedroom in Biloxi in 1872. That man, by the way, was never identified.

LUCILLE BALL

Like many of us, Lucille Ball experienced life as both sexes in her forty-two incarnations. In the 1700s, she was a man named Albert, born in Scotland to a cobbler and his wife, a seamstress. Albert was an only child, and his parents adored him, but they were poor and worked very long hours to make ends meet. He was fourteen when, eager to contribute to the family finances, he took a job as a janitor for a friend of his father's who happened to be a jeweler. He quickly showed an interest in making handcrafted jewelry and, with the shop owner's encouragement, began learning that art. His greatest fascination was with cameos. He studied everything about them, from their history to the skill needed to create them, and discovered to his delight that he had the enormous talent and the deft, steady hands necessary to carve beautiful cameos to add to the shop's inventory.

It was almost by accident that he developed a very specific specialty. A customer commissioned him to design a cameo resembling a detailed profile he'd drawn of his wife. Albert accomplished it with stunning accuracy, then made the cameo into a large, exquisite pendant, which the customer's wife loved and wore often. She also happened to be a cousin of a woman named

Charlotte, the consort to King George III. Charlotte admired her cousin's cameo so much that she commissioned one for herself. Albert's reputation and popularity eventually spread far and wide as he created cameos in the likenesses of the elite gentry in both England and France, making him a very wealthy man.

Albert never married; he was too eccentric and set in his ways for marriage, as far as he was concerned. He did, however, have a platonic female companion named Juditha throughout his adult life. They were mutually devoted to each other as quite close friends. They traveled together and attended social occasions together, and Albert took full financial and personal responsibility for Juditha when she became terminally ill with tuberculosis, moving her into his home and hiring twenty-four-hour care for her until the day she died.

Albert was seventy-two and living in a country manor on the North Sea when robbers broke into his home and, while searching for valuables, beat him to death in his bed.

He reunited with his companion Juditha in this most recent lifetime, when they were known as Lucille Ball and her daughter Lucie Arnaz.

Another of Lucille's pivotal incarnations took place in the early 1800s in Mississippi. Her name was Corinne.

Her mother died when Corinne was six months old, leaving the child in the care of her alcoholic father and her paternal grandparents. By the time she was four years old, Corinne had been enlisted in the family business: a kind of carnival–snake oil–evangelical sideshow that traveled throughout the South. Her grandfather sold supposed cure-all potions, her father preached the gospel, and a handful of "freaks" (a midget, a bearded lady, and a muscle man) performed to help attract crowds. Corinne happened to be double-jointed and became the show's contortionist-gymnast.

Corinne was utterly devoted to her father, who adored her. When he was sober, they had a very loving relationship. When he was drunk, he was abusive and then desperately remorseful, while his parents looked the other way and pretended nothing was wrong, in the interest of keeping the family business together. Corinne was still a child when she adopted the role of taking care of, cleaning up after, and comforting her father. She believed that his alcoholism was something that he couldn't help. She never held him accountable, even when he mistreated her. He died of liver failure when she was eleven, and she never recovered from losing him.

After her father's death, a new evangelist was recruited for the traveling sideshow, a fifty-two-year-old man named Pastor Luke, who claimed that God had come to him in a vision to tell him that he and Corinne were meant to be married. Corinne's grandparents gave their blessing (to secure Pastor Luke's commitment to their failing business), and Pastor Luke and Corinne became man and wife when she was thirteen years old. He was mean, morally bankrupt, and demanded her absolute, unconditional obedience. Her one source of happiness was the baby boy to whom she gave birth at the age of fourteen. Sadly, the baby gave Pastor Luke another weapon with which to threaten Corinne when she "misbehaved"—at every imagined failure to obey, he would promise to take her son away from her and give him to the highest-bidding family in whatever town the troupe happened to be passing through.

Finally, when Corinne was seventeen, she decided she had no intention of letting her son be raised in such a violent, angry household. So one night, while her husband was preaching to a small crowd in central Florida and her grandparents were onstage beside him, pretending to be healed by his divinely gifted hands, Corinne ran with her son to an abandoned horse barn she'd noticed when the sideshow had first arrived in the area. She and the boy were discovered the following day by the elderly woman who owned the barn, a kind, generous, childless widow, who took them into her home and invited them to stay. Corinne was as much of a godsend to this woman as the woman was to Corinne and her son; the woman fell ill shortly after she had embraced these strangers, and Corinne took wonderful care of her until she passed away two years later. The woman left her modest home to Corinne and her son, and they lived there together, keeping very much to themselves (in case Pastor Luke was still looking for them), until Corinne died from heart disease at the age of thirty-two.

While Lucie Arnaz was the only family member to reappear in Lucille Ball's latest incarnation, Lucille did bring with her an empathy for and extraordinary patience with flawed, alcoholic men; a sense of familiarity, when it came to entertaining; and a compromised heart, which gave out on her on April 26, 1989, at the age of seventy-seven. She will be back for two more lifetimes.

JACK KEVORKIAN

The controversial "Dr. Death," whose forty-second and final incarnation ended on June 3, 2011, had a series of past lives that make his fervent belief in the compassion of assisted suicide far more understandable, whether you share that belief or not.

One of those past lives that most profoundly influenced him took place in Germany in the late 1600s. His name was Hans, and he was born with a withered left leg. He had three strong, athletic, "normal" older brothers who were of great help on the family sugar beet farm. That his family essentially ignored him and seemed ashamed of him for something beyond his control—his impairment—was a source of enormous sadness for him, compounded by a conversation he had overheard between his mother and her pastor, a man whose philosophy was an unfortunate blend of Christianity and superstition.

"Your son Hans," the pastor had said, "is clearly being punished for sins he committed in a past life. I'm afraid he'll be forced to carry this curse for as long as he lives, as his means of atonement." Hans's mother bought every word of this nonsense and, from that moment on, treated her son as if he were cursed. While she saw to his most basic needs, she maintained a physical and emotional distance from him for the rest of his life. Hans, to his credit, never for a moment believed what the pastor had said and decided to make a success of himself, whether or not anyone else thought he could do it.

(It's worth emphasizing, by the way, that it takes an extraordinarily advanced soul to chart itself to be born with a physical or mental challenge. The souls who make that choice deserve our greatest generosity, admiration, and respect.)

From the time he was a child Hans's most treasured emotional outlet was a journal he kept under his mattress. In it, he expressed his deepest thoughts and honed his considerable writing talent. When he was sixteen, without telling anyone in his family, he submitted a writing sample to the owner of a local newspaper, a sample that described in an eloquent, heartfelt way his views on finding hope and productivity despite being physically challenged. His sample was quickly published and well received, and Hans was then hired to provide weekly articles for the paper on a variety of uplifting, inspiring subjects whose central theme was the incalculable value of human dignity.

The sad irony was that the young man who was writing articles on human dignity was living reclusively in a one-room flat above the newspaper owner's barn. He was completely estranged from his family, by this point, and relied on a boy who delivered the papers to the townspeople to bring him needed supplies. While he was gaining some notoriety for his articles, he was afraid that the fans of his articles would be disappointed if they saw the extent to which he was disfigured. Hans might not have been a happy man, but he was content to earn a modest living doing something he loved and inspiring people in the process.

One of those people he inspired was a lovely blond woman named Brigitte, who was eight years older than Hans and who happened to be blind. Her family had treated her with the same shameful disregard that Hans's family had treated him, and his articles about hope and dignity had made her believe for the first time in her life that she mattered, that having a physical challenge did not mean she had no value and no future.

Through a contact with the newspaper owner, and with a great deal of persistence, Brigitte finally managed to meet Hans in person. He thought she was beautiful. The great compassion behind his writing had already convinced her that he was beautiful as well. He told her in their first conversation about his withered leg, which made no more difference to her than her blindness made to him. Within a few months the two of them were married and moved to a modest house on the newspaper owner's property.

Hans became Brigitte's eyes. She became his mobility. And they loved each other very much. They had two sons, both of whom became doctors and took care of Hans after Brigitte died very suddenly of a ruptured appendix. As devastated as Hans was at losing her, all he had to do was look back on his many years with her, and at his two successful sons, to know that at the core of the joy he and his wife had known was the simple, essential dignity they'd given each other and, as a result, had found in themselves.

Hans died quietly in his sleep of a massive stroke at the age of seventy-nine.

The spirit we knew as Jack Kevorkian carried that same deep belief in human dignity into his next incarnation in England in the late 1700s. This time around his name was Paul. He was the son of an admiral in the Royal Navy, proud, able-bodied, and smart from the day he was born. He had a privileged, loving upbringing and a top-notch education, which prepared him to pursue his goal of following in his father's footsteps. Before entering the Royal Navy, he married his sister's best friend, a beautiful nursing student named Rachel, and the two of them set up housekeeping before he left for military training, looking forward to the long life and happy family they knew were waiting for them right around the corner.

It was during Paul's second month at sea, when he was only twenty-three years old, that a massive storm hit and a mast, swinging out of control, crashed into his back, shattered his spine, and paralyzed him from the neck down. Rachel devoted her life to caring for him, and Paul's family supported them financially, but Paul felt he was only alive on a technicality, so to speak, loathing every minute of being useless and of being a burden to his wife and family. Knowing that his body was broken beyond repair and that tomorrow and every day after was going to be exactly the same as yesterday and the day before, he silently prayed every night that he would die in his sleep.

Twelve long, hard years later, Paul finally asked Rachel a question he'd been thinking about for a very long time: "Do you love me enough to let me go?"

After several days of talking and thinking and crying and discussing it with Paul's family, Rachel left the hospital where she worked with a syringe full of drugs, and that night, with the family gathered beside his bed, Rachel gently helped Paul go Home, believing with all her heart—and his—that it was the greatest act of love she could offer him.

Paul, joyfully healthy, watched with infinite peace from the Other Side as Rachel remarried a year later and gave birth to twins, a girl and a boy, who became the light of her life, and his gratitude for her having set him free will last an eternity.

All things considered, then, unless we lived similar past lives ourselves, how can we possibly be surprised, or even judgmental, about the work to which Jack Kevorkian returned to dedicate himself for his last incarnation?

MARILYN MONROE

One of the most iconic movie stars of all time, the hauntingly unforgettable Marilyn Monroe, born Norma Jeane Baker, was only on her eighteenth incarnation when she left this world for the last time on August 5, 1962. Envied, even idolized as she was, she wrote a more difficult chart for herself than she could handle for her final life on earth, believing that because she'd written similar charts for herself before, she knew what to expect and could finally get it right this time.

Her childhood in a succession of orphanages and foster homes, because of the mental illness of one or both of her parents, was one she'd been through over and over again, leading to one incarnation after another of extraordinary drama. In Portugal, for example, in the mid-1600s, when she was called Joana, her schizophrenic father killed her mother and then held two-year-old Joana hostage for several hours until the police were able to rescue her. In the tragically mistaken belief that she'd undoubtedly inherited her father's insanity, she was handed over by the authorities to a children's asylum, where she was routinely medicated with opium to keep her quiet and controlled.

Eventually, when she was ten, she was sold to a traveling band of gypsies, who touted her as the world's youngest fortune-teller and taught her the tricks of the trade, from "table tipping" to removing imaginary curses to very adept pickpocketing. She despised every minute of it, but she had nowhere else to go and not a coin to her name, and she was assured repeatedly that if she tried to escape, they would find her and bring her back, no matter how far away she ran. They continued giving her opium, using it themselves and trading in it to supplement their income.

By the time Joana was fifteen she was resigned to her life of no structure, no love, no place to call home, and no pleasure that wasn't drug-induced. She had also grown into an ethereally beautiful young girl, who bore an uncanny resemblance to her mother. This only made her life more difficult—the more attention she attracted from the men in the troupe and in the towns to which they traveled, the more the women in the troupe resented her and wanted her gone. The men, though, were the ones with the power to decide who left and who stayed, and they weren't about to lose their star attraction. So for better or worse Joana was kept there, protected and increasingly pampered by the men in exchange for sex, while the women treated her with cruel disdain. Her favors were frequently sold to the locals as well, and she frankly thought no more of that than she thought of the other tricks of the trade she'd been taught and had come to equate with her value on this earth.

Early one morning, as the troupe was setting up camp in a small town on the German border, she noticed an older man standing some distance away, staring at her. Her first instinct was fear. The authorities had run them out of more towns throughout Europe than she could count, and occasionally there had been an arrest or even an execution or two when their thievery had caught up with them. The arrival of agents of the law always terrified her. But this man wasn't trying to interfere. Nor was he watching the troupe. His sole focus was on her. And the more she returned his gaze, the less afraid and more curious she got, until finally she moved close enough to him to hear him quietly say, "Joana? Is it you? My God, you look just like your mother."

It was her uncle, her mother's brother, who'd been looking for her since he had learned that his sister had been killed and her only child was gone. It had taken him years to track her down to the asylum where she'd been sent, only to be told that she was no longer there but had been "adopted" by a band of gypsies. He'd spent even more years traveling throughout the continent, searching for her in every gypsy camp he could find, until he'd finally accepted the impossible odds against finding her. That hadn't stopped him, though, from checking out every camp that arrived in his own area, and he was overwhelmed with joy and relief that he'd finally found her.

Joana was overwhelmed too. She hadn't known that she had any family left at all, let alone that someone in her family would have cared enough to look for her. Her uncle seemed kind and sincere and eager to help her, if she needed help, or just happy to get to know her, if she didn't. All she wanted, she told him, was a chance to get away from the gypsies and start a life in which she might finally have a future and some semblance of happiness, although she couldn't imagine what that might look like.

That night he helped her escape and took her to his small apartment above the modest cobbler shop he'd owned for thirty years. He was a widower, he told her, and his children were all grown and gone. He was hardly a wealthy man, but he would do his best to take care of her for as long as she wanted to stay—it was the least he could do for his only sister's daughter.

To her great credit, she felt compelled to warn him about something she'd come to accept as fact, after hearing it all her life: it was probable that she'd inherited her father's mental illness, in which case she might become a danger to him or a burden, without meaning to. If, knowing that, he would rather she left, she would understand.

He smiled and wisely pointed out that if she really were mentally ill, she probably wouldn't have had the insight to be aware of it, let alone to tell him about it. He was willing to take his chances. He was every bit as kind as he seemed, and for the first time in her memory, Joana felt a connection, a sense of belonging, and even a glimmer of hope.

It only lasted a few short days. Just as they'd promised they would if she tried to run away, the men of the gypsy troupe tracked her down, killing her uncle when he tried to stop them from taking her. She was in no shape to put up a fight, going through excruciating withdrawal from her lifelong opium addiction by the time they found her. Between the cold-turkey withdrawal, the anguish of seeing her newfound family member and savior killed, and the stress of being taken back to a life she despised, her heart gave out before they reached the camp. Joana went Home, grateful to leave this earth.

The only person Marilyn Monroe brought with her from that or any other incarnation was her uncle, who was with Marilyn briefly as her husband but more importantly as a good, loving friend throughout her life and long after, when his name was Joe DiMaggio.

The recurring patterns in Marilyn Monroe's eighteen incarnations will always fascinate me. Not once in any of her lives did she have children, for example, either out of concern that she might have inherited and could therefore pass along a psychiatric problem or because not once did she have a childhood that she would have wished on anyone, let alone on a child of her own. Time and time again she was taught that the key to any kind of security was through male attention and approval, and never did any of her lifetimes offer her any sense of structure or discipline. Substance abuse was an issue in twelve of her eighteen lives. And maybe most important of all, there was no incarnation in which she was encouraged and guided toward finding her own identity and her own spiritual core. I couldn't help but think, when I'd finished studying her difficult journey in this world, that it was no wonder she'd had it with this place and had decided to stay Home from now on.

VINCENT PRICE

The iconic actor whose image and voice became synonymous with the macabre completed his forty-eighth and final incarnation in 1993. His ability to frighten audiences around the world, and then essentially spoof his career in his later years, belied a gentle, refined man who studied art at Yale, was a gourmet cook, and very publicly and passionately spoke out against the poison of prejudice. A past life in Kansas was a perfect preface to his last multifaceted lifetime.

He was born in the 1830s. His name was Alfred, one of two sons born to a farmhand and his wife, a Sunday school teacher and homemaker, who also created and sold extraordinary handmade quilts. Alfred and his older brother, Benton, were smart, outgoing, popular boys who loved working with their father as he traveled from farm to farm, wherever his help was needed, for enough of an hourly wage to modestly support his family.

Alfred was in his mid-teens when he was kicked in the face by a horse while helping his father with a blacksmithing job. It was uncertain, at first, whether or not he would live, but after several weeks, the danger of a concussion or brain damage had passed and he was back to normal, with the exception of a very badly disfigured face that couldn't be healed or reconstructed. The only way he could possibly have covered his wounds was with a full mask, which made him feel even more self-conscious than his disfigurement, so he let the world see him and hoped for the best.

The reactions from those around him devastated him. Longtime friends turned away or cruelly teased him. Strangers either turned away or gaped with repulsed incredulity. Teachers suggested to his parents that he be schooled at home, because his simple presence in classes was too disruptive. Children, whom he loved, were frightened of him and ran away. He'd always dreamed of being a preacher, with a wife and children of his own, but that dream slipped farther and farther away with each new stare of revulsion or child cowering at the sight of him. He wished people would take the time and patience to realize that, inside, he was still exactly the same person he'd always been, the same person they'd once liked and gravitated toward.

His parents and brother, thank God, were supportive, and when his mother received a modest inheritance after the death of her parents, she bought Alfred a small two-room cabin of his own within walking distance of the family house, respecting his wish to find a way to become as independent as possible and somehow earn his own living.

He became understandably reclusive, which, human nature being what it is, gradually made him the target of gossip, speculation, and children's scary stories. He'd gone insane, some said. He was performing perverse acts behind those heavily draped windows, said others.

He was kidnapping neighborhood children, killing them, cooking them, and eating them for dinner, little brothers and sisters whispered to each other in bed after the lights were turned out. It was horribly cruel, especially when it was aimed at a young man who was doing everything in his power to attract absolutely no attention at all.

His resolve to be a productive, contributing member of society never dimmed in the slightest, and slowly but surely possibilities began occurring to him. At his suggestion, his father and brother began bringing him carts and wheelbarrows in need of repair from the farms where they worked. Alfred, who'd always been talented with his hands, could fix them perfectly and then be paid whatever money his father and brother would have made for the job. That evolved into another idea: they brought him salvaged wheelbarrows, carts, wagons, wood, and metal, out of which Alfred taught himself to craft beautifully made toys and dollhouses. These his family quietly and anonymously left, at his request, on the doorsteps of struggling families on Christmas Eve.

Alfred's skill evolved into another brainstorm for the benefit of the local children. With the help of his parents and brother, who brought whatever food and supplies he needed, he began studying writing and art, voraciously reading every book on the arts that they could find for him and developing his own considerable skills with oil paints. In less than a year he'd created a collection of exquisite marionettes with incredibly expressive faces and extraordinarily elaborate hand-painted outfits. He wrote plays for his marionettes to perform, lighthearted plays with messages of kindness, tolerance, and generosity, and built a colorful little stage on which the plays would be performed. Then, wearing a friendly, funny mask he had designed for himself, a mask behind which he felt comfortable, in the context of being a master of ceremonies for children's entertainment, he began putting on puppet shows that became wildly successful with families throughout the area. Soon, he expanded his repertoire and his marionette collection to include puppet shows that depicted everything from Bible stories to the life stories of the various artists he'd been studying, so that the local children—many of whom had never been taught to read or write—found themselves excitedly curious about the lives and works of Rembrandt, Da Vinci, and Michelangelo. His masked proximity to the children made it possible for him to find out the dates of their birthdays, and on the appropriate mornings, they would wake up to find art books, paints, and brushes or toys on their doorsteps, delivered in the dark of night.

When he wasn't busy performing and creating surprises for children, Alfred spent his long, reclusive hours cooking for himself and his family or creating beautiful oil paintings, employing techniques he had learned from his many art books. His brother enjoyed traveling throughout the area, selling Alfred's paintings, and Alfred enjoyed saving up the proceeds and repaying every dime that his mother had invested in him from her inheritance all those years ago.

Alfred was the first of the family to pass away. He died quietly and suddenly in his sleep at the age of forty-one of an undiagnosed blood clot in his lungs, a peaceful ending to the story of the scariest man in town. He had turned a potentially tragic, bitter life into a full, joyful, generous one, which prepared him perfectly to come back one more time as a man called Vincent Price.

ANWAR EL-SADAT

Anwar el-Sadat's most recent incarnation as the president of Egypt and winner of the 1978 Nobel Peace Prize was his forty-ninth and his last. I have to admit, I hold a special place in my heart for Sadat. He was one of my heroes. Part of my innate sense of connection to him is my love of Egypt, where I lived a few of my happier incarnations, but there was also the fact that I thought of him as a kind, fair, spiritual man who truly believed in equality.

I knew—*not politically*, I can't stress that enough, but purely psychically—that something horrible was going to happen on October 6, 1981, at Sadat's military review. I still remember, as clearly as if it had happened this morning, trying to get in touch with his aides to warn him not to go. I did successfully contact Nancy Reagan and advised her that under no circumstances should President Reagan attend. In fact, the Secret Service called me to ask what I knew and how I knew it. It came as a sickening shock when the breaking news hit that Anwar el-Sadat had been assassinated that day, and what a loss to the world it was.

Sadat's deep passion for his country had its beginning when he was one of the chief advisors to King Tutankhamen (originally Tutankhaten). During his brief reign, with Sadat by his side (then known as Seth), King Tut reunited Egypt with its traditional polytheism, which had been banned by his predecessor, Akhenaten, who had insisted on the worship of only one god, Aten, the sun god. In the process of dismissing the belief in several gods, Akhenaten had had their temples destroyed, but on ascending to the throne King Tut had them restored, along with their images and privileges. He also abandoned Akhenaten's royal home in Tell el-Amarna and chose instead to live in Memphis, which was the administrative capital of ancient Egypt. King Tut was only nineteen years old when he died and was succeeded by Ay, one of the king's most powerful advisors.

On the death of Tutankhamen, in fear of being executed (as had happened to several of his colleagues in the king's inner circle), Seth slipped quietly away to Israel, where he lived a modest, almost solitary life, disguising his identity with a simple change of his name. While he never married, he adopted several children from local orphanages, raised them with gentle, loving care, and taught them theology and the principles of peace and nonviolence.

When Seth reached the age of sixty and knew his health was failing, he set out on foot to return to his beloved homeland. He was only two miles from the Israeli-Egyptian border when he collapsed and died from exposure and dehydration.

One of the most remarkable facts about Sadat's past lives is his passionate loyalty to Egypt. I've done thousands and thousands of past-life regressions with clients and studied more past lives through Francine than I can count, and Sadat is the first and only spirit I've found who lived all but one of his incarnations in the same country.

The one exception was a lifetime in Iran. He was born in Shiraz in the early 1820s and was a close childhood friend of Siyyid Ali Muhammad, who was later known as the Báb, a descendant of Muhammad prophesied to return to earth to restore the unity of the human race and the belief in only one god. Sadat, then known as Farid, followed his friend, believing him to be a manifestation of God and drawn to his message of peace and unity, which ultimately became the core of the Bahá'i faith. As the popularity of the Báb and his disciples spread across Iran and Iraq, they became a threat to the Islamic government. In 1848, two years before the Báb was executed by firing squad on the order of Prime Minister Amir Kabir, Farid was surrounded by a small group of Islamic loyalists in the streets of Tabriz. They demanded that he renounce his faith in the Báb and his teachings. Farid refused and remained fearless, peaceful, and unrepentant as the loyalists stoned him to death, as unafraid to die for what he believed as he was in his final incarnation as Anwar el-Sadat.

KATHARINE HEPBURN

Katharine Hepburn's most recent incarnation, which ended on June 29, 2003, as the result of an inoperable tumor in her neck, was her fiftieth and her last. And while it might be tempting to look for Spencer Tracy in some of those past lives, because their relationship was so strong and inevitable, he can't be found, and for a simple reason: Katharine Hepburn and Spencer Tracy are soul mates, and it's *very* rare for soul mates to spend a lifetime on earth together. Soul mates are twin souls created by God, mirror images of each other, with an extraordinary connection between them. While they're not inseparable on the Other Side, they're rarely apart. For them to incarnate together as well is generally thought to be just plain redundant, which makes Tracy and Hepburn even more exceptional than we knew them to be.

That's not to say, though, that no one from Katharine's past lives played a significant role in her final life on earth.

In one of her earlier incarnations, Katharine—whose name was Mahvash—was a dancer in the Persian court of King Solomon. Her talent and beauty were greatly admired, but she was a source of some frustration to the king for her disinterest in being one of his concubines. Fiercely independent even then, she insisted on living her own simple life with her brother, Avan, a blacksmith, in a modest, meticulous flat far from the luxuries the king had to offer. In her opinion, there was no greater luxury than freedom, and hers was not for sale. She taught dance. She was a brilliant horse-woman who often won horse races against her brother, with whom she shared a deep mutual admiration. The two of them also shared a fascination with astronomy, literature, and sculpture. While each of them had their share of lovers, they preferred each other's company above all others, and neither of them ever married.

She died of blood poisoning at the age of forty-nine, content with the life she'd lived as Mahvash. (She and Avan would happily meet again on earth on May 12, 1907, the day she was born as Katharine Hepburn. She instantly recognized her father, Dr. Thomas Hepburn, as the brother she'd once adored.)

Katharine's life in Delaware in the early 1800s was a difficult one, though it started out with great prom-ise. Sarah, as she was known then, was married at the age of sixteen to a man named Benjamin, the wealthy owner of two successful inns on the Atlantic Seaboard. They were deeply in love and committed to each other. They planned to have a large family and to expand Benjamin's business holdings, taking full advantage of his investment capital and her innately sharp, shrewd financial and real estate instincts.

Sarah was pregnant with their first child when Benjamin left for a trip to explore available land in Maryland, which they were hoping would be the perfect site for a new inn. Tragically, Benjamin never returned, and Sarah would never learn what happened to him. He'd been robbed of his travel bags and murdered on the third day of his journey with no way to identify him let alone notify his next of kin.

Another tragedy struck six months later. Due to the incompetency of her midwife, Sarah's first and only child, a son named Ephraim, suffered brain and neurological damage as a result of oxygen deprivation. Sarah devoted herself to caring for him, especially sharing her love of literature with him; she would sit tirelessly beside his bed reading to him, and whether or not he understood what he was hearing, the sound of her voice soothed him and brought him comfort. "How else will he ever know these beautiful words," she would say, "if he doesn't hear them from me?"—a question that also lay at the heart of her lifetime as the actress named Katharine Hepburn.

Ephraim was fifteen years old when his compromised immune system was unable to successfully fight off influenza during an epidemic that had swept through New England. Sarah's grief over the loss of her beloved son left her desolate and in serious doubt about her faith in God, unable to understand how a kind, loving Father could allow as sweet and innocent a soul as Ephraim to live such a harshly challenged life.

God, however, doesn't require that we believe in Him. He never stops believing in us, and our service to humankind is always a form of worship, whether that is our intention or not. What Sarah did with the rest of her life was a pure expression of godliness, even though in her heart she was simply honoring her son's memory. She became a midwife, to prevent other mothers and newborns from the cruel, avoidable challenges she and Ephraim had been through. She was tireless, she was comforting, she was fearless, and she was brilliant, never losing a single patient. She saved many lives throughout the Northeast, and her reputation attracted the attention of several doctors in the area to whom she became a trusted colleague and consultant.

Sarah lived to be seventy-one, dying alone of emphysema in the home she'd shared with her husband and son. She asked for no help at the end of her life and, unable to continue her work as a midwife, felt that she was of no further use and was ready to go.

Katharine Hepburn met Ephraim again in her final incarnation, in the persona of her older brother Tom. Tom was a victim of a powerful cell-memory trauma from his brief lifetime of being mentally and physically impaired. Katharine never fully recovered from his suicide when he was, not coincidentally, fifteen years old. Her almost pathological need for privacy was in direct conflict with her determination to be a gifted actress and share "beautiful words" with millions of people, as she'd once shared them with Ephraim. The fierce independence she'd brought from many of her past lives often created conflicts between her and the studios that hired her. To help her successfully resolve those conflicts and accomplish the goals she'd charted for herself for her last life on earth, she saw to it that her soul mate, Spencer Tracy, was right by her side.

DEAN MARTIN

One of the most remarkable things about actor-singer Dean Martin, the "King of Cool," is that he frequently chose a loner theme for his fifty-one incarnations but was, more often than not, born into very large families. Those souls with a loner theme, no matter how populated their lives or how public their careers might make them, tend to require their share of private time, or at most, time with just one or two other people with whom they're especially close.

This was true in his unremarkable life on a farm in sixth-century China, when he was one of thirteen children (including a brother who, in his most recent incarnation, was his Rat Pack partner Sammy

Davis Jr.) and would often wander away from home for days at a time for no other reason than simply needing some uninterrupted hours to himself. It was also true in his fifty-first and final life as an entertainer; when he hadn't been performing, he preferred playing golf and watching television to partying. And it was certainly true during his life in the American colony of Virginia in the mid-1700s.

His name was David then, and he was the youngest of eleven children born to a fairly wealthy couple, who'd traveled to the colonies from Suffolk, England. Incredibly, Sammy Davis Jr. was one of his brothers in that life as well, but there was a twelve-year age difference between them and they were never especially close. The only sibling with whom he was very close—whom he idolized—was his brother John, who was just one year older than David. They were each other's favorite playmates, best friends, and co-conspirators in pranks against their brothers and sisters, and each other's most loyal, vigilant protector. "Hurt him and you'll have me to reckon with" seemed to be their motto from the moment they met, when David was about thirty minutes old.

Most of the brothers and sisters were excellent students with very specific career goals. Three of them attended Harvard, while John was following in their father's footsteps as a silversmith. But David, though bright and not at all lazy, didn't find a direction that inspired him until he was in town one day, on his way to his father's shop, and came across a street puppeteer. He delighted in the man's improvisational freedom and his ability to attract and amuse generous, appreciative passersby. Without confiding in anyone but John about his plans, David began working on a street-performance act of his own, focusing primarily on his longtime hobby of magic, with a few songs and dance steps thrown in as filler between tricks. John not only kept his brother's secret, he also helped him refine the act (in their amateur version of the word "refine") until it was really very entertaining, and within a few weeks David was making a modest living and thoroughly enjoying himself.

A young, attractive woman named Becky worked in a bakery near the corner where David performed. She began sneaking him what occasional snacks she could several times throughout the day. It only enhanced her infatuation of him that he always insisted on paying for the snacks. He developed feelings for her too, and very slowly, very properly the beginnings of a sweet romance took shape.

Almost overnight, it seemed, everything changed, thanks to the Revolutionary War. John and David, swept up in the growing atmosphere of patriotism and the call to arms, became excited about the idea of being minutemen together, fighting side by side for their country's independence. Their parents and their siblings were proud of them, sad about their choice, but understanding, and the young men promptly enlisted. David said goodbye to Becky with a promise that when he returned they would pick up where they had left off. And the town threw a celebratory farewell celebration for John, David, and the other young men in the area who were marching off to war.

They had made plans to leave the following day, but David woke with a raging fever and headache. He was devastated when he was diagnosed with smallpox, for which he had to be immediately isolated. John was unable to even say goodbye to his brother before he left on his own, confident that David would follow as soon as he had fully recovered.

David was on the mend several weeks later when word came that John had been one of the casualties at Valley Forge. Family and friends were distraught, of course, but David was disconsolate, his incalculable loss compounded by a severe case of survivor's guilt, doomed to wonder for the rest of his life whether he could have saved John if he'd been there beside him, where he belonged. Unable to eat, sleep, or function,

David checked himself into an institution, fully prepared to die there and not caring if he did.

Becky began visiting him, loving him, comforting him, and expecting nothing from him. David tried to push her away. He couldn't offer her a future, he told her. He couldn't in good conscience ask her to stay with him when he had no reason to believe he'd ever be happy again, let alone be able to make her happy. She understood and assured him that there were no strings attached to her wanting to spend time with him. She was where she knew she belonged, and if the time came for her to move on, she would. But for the moment, if it would be all right with him, she wanted to stay.

It took months for David to be able to return to some form of normalcy. His depression never quite lifted, but with Becky's gentle diligence and his eventual desire to live, he eventually left the institution, and the two of them were married. He did love her, and he was enormously grateful to her for accepting him for exactly who he was and respecting his need for time to himself, without being offended by it or trying to change him. By now she owned the bakery where she'd once worked. She had turned it into a thriving business so was able and perfectly willing to support the two of them. But after a couple of years, David came to believe that John would never have approved of his sitting around doing nothing and would have been especially disappointed that David had abandoned the street performances John had enjoyed so much. Slowly at first, David revived his act. He placed himself in front of Becky's shop, where they could attract business for each other. And the community, sympathetic to David's loss and his struggle to recover, and genuinely happy to see him perform again, cheered him on with even more enthusiasm and generosity than they had before John's death.

David and Becky lived a long, contented life together before he succumbed to lung disease, his immune system never having fully renewed itself after the smallpox. He was seventy-one when he died, and he was buried, as he requested, next to his beloved brother.

David, Becky, and John met again in what would be all of their last incarnations. Becky returned as Jeanne Biegger, who Dean Martin was married to for twenty-three years before they divorced and then, after a three-year separation, reconciled. She was at his bedside when he went Home in 1995 after respiratory failure. As for John, he came back as Dean and Jeanne's son, Dean Paul Martin, who was killed in a jet fighter crash in 1987 during his service with the California Air National Guard, a tragedy from which Dean never recovered. Whether he consciously remembered or not, he wasn't just mourning the unspeakable death of his child; he was also reliving the long-ago loss of the brother he had adored. When Dean died, he wandered as an earthbound in darkness and grief until finally his brother and son, Dean Paul, reached out to him from the Other Side and brought him Home to stay.

FARRAH FAWCETT

Iconically beautiful, award-winning actress Farrah Fawcett completed her twenty-first incarnation in June of 2009, and she's decided she'll be back one more time, in 2026, to become an oncologist in Sweden. She'd been building toward her most recent lifetime for centuries, most specifically in the lifetime that immediately preceded it, in Brazil in the early 1900s.

Her name was Juliana, and as in her latest incarnation, she was a feminine, charismatic beauty from the day she was born, with jet-black hair, blue-green eyes, and perfect features. She grew up on a cattle ranch leased from one of the wealthiest, most prestigious families in the country. Her parents doted on her, but they were status-conscious social climbers—the kind of people who today would sell their souls, or their daughter, for their own TV reality show. They'd always felt as if they were a bit on the outside looking in when it came to the truly elite crowd to which they aspired. The more they were excluded from the A-list, the more determined they became to be included. As Juliana became more and more spectacular with each passing year, her parents began to believe that she might be their elusive ticket to those best-of-the-best parties and events, if only they could see to it that she caught the eye of their version of Mr. Right.

After years of sending her to the most prestigious boarding and finishing schools, they got their wish, and then some. Their magnificent Juliana, now perfectly polished with impeccable manners and social graces, attracted the attention and then the heart of none other than the son of the family who owned the property they were leasing. His name was Marcelo. He was ten years older than Juliana, as handsome as she was beautiful, wealthy, spoiled, and entitled. He was also a skillful ballroom dancer and dinner partner, and had a carefully cultivated charm. He was one of the most desirable bachelors in Brazil and was now single again, after a brief marriage had ended in an annulment so as not to offend his Catholic parents, who found divorce distasteful even more than they found it sacrilegious.

Because it meant so much to her parents, Juliana immersed herself in her newfound relationship with

Marcelo and did her best to fall in love with him. And sure enough, in the blink of an eye, her parents found themselves on the A-list, invited to all the glittering parties and social events they'd yearned to attend. To add to the embarrassment of riches into which their daughter had ushered them, on the day of Juliana and Marcelo's fairy-tale wedding, their landlords, and new in-laws, elevated their status from tenants to partners in the ranch property they'd leased and handsomely maintained for two decades.

But three years into her marriage, Juliana reluctantly admitted to her parents that, despite her attempts to hide it, she was desperately unhappy. Marcelo, she'd discovered, had married her more as a trophy than as a woman he loved and wanted to spend his life with. He was cold and distant when they weren't out in public. He was cruel, sulking, and impossible when he didn't get his way or when Juliana wasn't instantly compliant with whatever he said, no matter how insipid or wrong it might be. He'd never actually hit her, but he'd made it clear that he wouldn't hesitate "if she pushed him too far." He was also utterly controlling, demanding to know where she was at every moment. If she spent more time away from the house than he felt she should have, such as riding her beloved horses to let off steam, he would fly into a rage that could last for hours, accusing her of sneaking off to meet a lover and calling her a whore. Perhaps her greatest disappointment was that even though he'd assured her during their courtship that he wanted children as desperately as she did, he actually had no intention of being a father. He didn't care for children, would certainly never tolerate a girl child, and would demand that any girls be put up for adoption. Plus, he couldn't bear the thought of Juliana "disfiguring" her body with a pregnancy. Juliana had tried everything she could think of to make this marriage work, but she was sure that Marcelo was as miserable as she was. She decided it would be best for the two of them to move on with their lives, as far away from each other as possible.

It's an understatement to say that her parents were not supportive. In fact, they were ashamed of her, they said, and desperately disappointed in her. Why would it even occur to her to let go of this wonderful man, a man any other woman in all of Brazil would give anything just to be near, a man they'd spent a fortune grooming Juliana to attract, a man who—along with his family— had been so kind and generous to them? She was never to let such insanity enter her mind again. If Juliana was not making him happy then she would just have to try harder. And if he wasn't making her happy, there was clearly something terribly wrong with her.

There was indeed something terribly wrong with Juliana. It took hold slowly when Juliana, feeling alone and helpless, returned to Marcelo and resigned herself to staying in her marriage, whether it worked or not. She began losing an alarming amount of weight, feeling oddly lethargic, and having no appetite at all. By the time she noticed the lump in her left breast, it was too late—she'd developed what would today be recognized as stage-four breast cancer.

Marcelo, thoroughly inconvenienced by this disruption in his otherwise smooth-sailing life, arranged for a private room at a nearby sanitarium so he wouldn't have a sick wife underfoot. He checked her in under an assumed name to prevent unwanted negative attention drawn to either him or his family. Juliana's mother, who considered herself a very religious woman, was angry that Juliana's illness was threatening to "ruin everything." She took the position that God had inflicted His cancer on Juliana as a way of punishing her for her ingratitude for all that she'd been given, and that Juliana should be ashamed of herself and tell no one how ill she was. Juliana's father, who'd learned decades earlier that no good could come from displeasing his wife, simply kept his mouth shut and cooperated with his wife's refusal to visit their daughter and risk God's wrath by sympathizing with her.

In her brief time at the sanitarium, Juliana became acquainted with several of the other terminally ill women with whom she would share a few hours every afternoon on the hospital grounds. Those hours were the closest she ever came to having genuine friends who appreciated her kindness and concern, and gave it back in return. No matter what their social status when they were hospitalized, they'd all experienced feeling alone and frightened from time to time in their lives and, in many cases, were blamed for what was happening to them and ostracized by their families rather than embraced. Until they'd met and begun to unite in their common pain, they'd never truly opened up to anyone. This group of women had long, cathartic talks about everything from abusive marriages to drug and alcohol problems to profound loneliness to a feeling that, in the busy-ness and drama of their lives, they'd inadvertently wandered away from God. It was as eye-opening as it was emotionally healing for Juliana to hear that other women had been through the same fears, self-doubt, and unhappiness that she'd experienced. In offering compassion and reassurance to the others, Juliana found that she received even more reassurance than she gave.

When she left that lifetime at the age of thirty-two, her hospital bed surrounded by her newfound friends, Juliana promised herself that she would come quickly back to this world and create a voice for herself by becoming famous, then use that voice to reach out to women like those at the sanitarium—women like herself—to make sure that, no matter what the superficial appearances to the contrary might be and no matter what personal hardship life might have dealt them, they weren't alone.

For the record, Juliana brought no one from that incarnation into her lifetime as Farrah Fawcett.

BORIS KARLOFF

In his fifty-fifth and final incarnation, Boris Karloff, the Master of Horror, continued the life theme that he had worked for so many lifetimes to perfect, the somewhat unexpected theme of rescuer.

Rescuers are exactly what the word implies: those who gravitate toward victims, wanting to help them and save them, even when the victims have created their own crises or don't see themselves as needing to be saved. Rescuers are highly empathetic and are typically at their strongest in the presence of the weakest or most helpless. They can find themselves being victimized, if they're not vigilant about the motives and actions of those they're trying to rescue.

Karloff's life in Sweden in the 1600s was a perfect example of the victimization of a rescuer. His name was Halsten, and he and his three brothers had all followed in their father's footsteps to become highly respected attorneys. They were as wealthy and privileged as they were hardworking, but they never took advantage of their elevated social positions or their potential influence with the judges who tried their cases. Even if they'd been tempted, they knew their father would have been the first to see to it that they never practiced law again, rather than allow them to compromise the integrity of the family name.

Halsten, in particular, didn't hesitate to take on pro bono cases, if he believed in the innocence of the accused. He was in his mid-twenties when he met a client who would change his life: Emma. She was nineteen and suspected of the stabbing death of her father, a man who was known to be cruel and aggressive, and with a hair-trigger temper. When Halsten met the lovely, desperately frightened young woman, his heart went out to her.

The only three people in the house on the night of the murder, Emma had told him, were her father, her high-strung mother, who had hated her father, and herself. She had awoken the next morning to find that her father had been killed in his sleep and her mother was hysterical, claiming that he'd attacked her and she'd had no choice but to defend herself. Within days her mother had changed her story and blamed the murder on Emma.

Halsten had little trouble getting Emma exonerated. With the two women blaming each other, there was no way to clearly establish which of them had committed the murder, so neither of them was ever convicted. In the lengthy process of defending her and hearing about the difficult life Emma had had with parents who were so unhappy and combative, Halsten fell in love with her and wanted to give her the wonderful future he felt she deserved.

They were married within a year. A year after that, Emma gave birth to a beautiful, healthy son. They named him Rolf, and Halsten had never known such joy as he discovered when he became a father. His career kept him away from home for hours and hours each day, and because Rolf's birth had been a difficult one, Emma was overwhelmed. She was still regaining her health while at the same time trying to care for a newborn. So Halsten happily offered to hire a live-in nanny. To his surprise and concern, Emma wanted no one but her mother. Her mother, she pointed out, was all alone now and, without her nightmare of a husband, wanted a chance to make amends with her daughter and grandson and become part of a happy family for the first time. As for the murder of her father, Emma felt it was a one-time act of sheer desperation and self-defense, on her mother's part, and Emma would never let her mother near Rolf if she weren't completely convinced that he'd be safe.

To make Emma happy, and because her mother was very attentive to Emma and Rolf, Halsten welcomed her into the household. Things went fairly well for several months, although the two women seemed to be teaming up to make a lot of decisions about the house and the baby without taking his input into account. Plus, the amount of time he was getting to spend with his son was gradually diminishing. There was no doubt that Emma's health was improving, but she was becoming increasingly moody and argumentative with Halsten. She was perfectly willing to start petty arguments with him and yell at him, and her mother chimed in to defend her, which the very even-tempered Halsten found unacceptable, especially when acted out in front of Rolf.

The more the tension in the household escalated, despite Halsten's best efforts to the contrary, the more concerned he became about his son's emotional well-being and his wife and his mother-in-law's mental stability. He finally sat down with Emma in private one evening and suggested that, since they'd been happy until her mother had come to live with them, and since Emma was in good health again, maybe it was time for her mother to live elsewhere and ease the stressful atmosphere in which their son was being raised. He would buy her mother a home nearby, and they'd still see each other regularly, but clearly something needed to be done. Emma apologized, thanked him for his patience and generosity toward her mother, and promised she'd talk to her the very next morning.

Halsten arrived home late the next afternoon to discover that his wife, his mother-in-law, his son, all their belongings, and the substantial amount of money he had kept in the house were gone. He was frantic, devastated, and of course primarily concerned for Rolf. He took full advantage of his connections and influence in an effort to track them down and reunite with his son, and the longer he searched unsuccessfully, the more determined he became. Unfortunately, he knew that with the help of the financial resources they'd stolen from him, there was no limit to where they might have gone.

His search continued for eight long, fruitless, heartbreaking years, but giving up was not an option. He couldn't live with the idea of never seeing his son again, and whether or not he could legally punish his wife and mother-in-law was almost beside the point. It's impossible to guess if he would ever have found them had it not been for the woman who arrived at his door one day and said, "I understand you've been looking for your child, and I know where he is."

Her name was Sonia. She was the biological daughter of Emma's father by his first wife, who'd passed away when Sonia was two years old. When her father had remarried, her new stepmother had considered Sonia to be an unwelcome reminder that her husband had once loved another woman. At her insistence, Sonia had been sent away to Belgium, to be raised by her maternal grandparents. She'd had a wonderful life there and married very well, successfully putting her past behind her, until recently. With no warning, her stepmother, a stepsister she'd never met (Emma), and a nine-year-old boy (Rolf) had shown up on her doorstep in search of money. It was the first Sonia had heard that her father had been murdered. The two women had tried their best to charm Sonia, but whether they meant to or not, the more they had talked, the more they had revealed.

Sonia had surmised that they'd plotted together to kill her father, who'd become an obstacle, and in such a way that neither of them could be prosecuted. When it had become apparent that Halsten was a kind, empathetic man, Emma had set her sights on him and then seen to it that her mother would come to live with them, so the two of them could ultimately run off with his child and his money. They had claimed that Halsten had been abusive to both Emma and Rolf, not realizing the contradiction in portraying him also as a kind, empathetic man. They were now out of money, with nowhere to stay and a nine-year-old child to care for.

Sonia had refused to give them money but, out of concern for Rolf, had allowed them to spend the night. The next morning the two women were gone, along with some of Sonia's husband's money, but they'd left Rolf behind. Sonia had gleaned enough information from them to track Halsten down and wanted to meet him before she simply handed over the boy, in order to satisfy herself that this home was a safe place for him to live. She now could see that it was.

Halsten returned to Belgium with Sonia to retrieve his son, and he devoted the rest of his life and law career to fighting for children's rights. Rolf ultimately became an officer in the Royal Swedish Navy, while Halsten died at the age of fifty-three from a fall that had shattered his spine and fractured his skull.

The Master of Horror, Boris Karloff, continued his long-established traits of kindness and gentility throughout his remaining lifetimes, along with having a recurring back pain as well as a rescuer's concern for the welfare of children. Sonia—the woman who had reunited him with his son—returned to Karloff's life as his daughter, Sara. Karloff also met Emma again, as a fan who wanted very much to start a relationship with him, but "something" told him to have nothing to do with her and he successfully discouraged her. She moved along to another actor we won't name, for obvious legal reasons, but who had the misfortune to marry her and didn't survive the marriage.

COCO CHANEL

The iconic designer Coco Chanel spent her forty-four incarnations fluctuating between male and female personas, never quite sure which gender gave her more of an advantage in this world. At the very least, it was her comfort with both genders that inspired her, while on earth as a brilliant female designer, to create the trademark women's fashions that hinted at the influence of menswear without losing any femininity. In the far bigger picture, her past lives, including her most celebrated one, have added up to a troubled spirit that still has two more incarnations to go before it's completed its journey on earth. Male or female, Coco Chanel has had a long history of being in power and feeling entitled to that power. While that has led to meteoric success, it's also led to a quickness to judge and a combativeness in the face of perceived threats and slights, which she'll be working to overcome when she returns.

One of her first lives as a male was spent as a rising Mayan leader in AD 14. His name was Balam. His mother, who claimed to be gifted with divine visions, taught her son from birth that he was superior and that he must become accustomed to insisting on absolute obedience from those who were inferior to him, or he would never be the great leader her visions predicted or the great leader his father had been. His father had been a brave chieftain, she had lied, who had died in battle before Balam was born and was now one of the most powerful of all the Mayan gods of nature. (The truth was that his father was a potter, a man she had barely known, who had given her money when he'd learned she was pregnant, and then disappeared.)

Balam was incredibly bright and might actually have been a great leader, if he'd learned to earn respect instead of demanding it. He was clever enough to seek out and ingratiate himself to those in power, who were impressed with the fabricated lineage he believed to be true and with the exquisite garments his mother had managed to procure. He rose through the ranks of leadership based on appearances, brains, and a false reputation, and he fully embraced the Mayan pantheistic worship of nature, in which his imaginary father was among the revered. Balam demanded, and was given, a palatial home, fully staffed with servants to whom he was as cruel as he'd been taught to be. Leaders regularly met there in private, to strategize and to enjoy Balam's studied, elitist hospitality.

Balam began to notice a dark-haired, exquisitely beautiful, and elegantly dressed young woman dripping in fine jewels. While not quite stalking him, she seemed to be deliberately appearing at places Balam was known to frequent and then would watch him with unapologetic interest. Her beauty, her obvious status, and her open attraction to him drew him to her like a magnet. He was even more intrigued to discover that she was quietly, demurely mysterious about her past, except to say that she was a daughter of royalty and the recent widow of a much older land baron. She was a dream come true for Balam, and he promptly took her into his home and into his bed.

As soon as Balam had fallen asleep, after they made love, the woman drew a dagger from the folds of her gown and plunged it into his back, killing him instantly. She then quickly slipped out the door. The servants, who hated their master, simply packed their meager belongings and returned to their lives elsewhere without reporting his death. So it was his mother who found his body, days later.

Ironically, the beautiful young woman had been neither a daughter of royalty nor married to a land baron. She had actually been a Spanish peasant, recruited because of her looks and her need for money and then dressed appropriately for the charade. She had been assigned to eliminate this young man, who was rumored to be ascending to power, all in anticipation of the Spanish invasion of the Mayans.

Coco Chanel's cell memory, incidentally, retained the pain of that wound through every one of her subsequent lifetimes; she suffered from backaches in her later years.

In the mid-1700s she was a woman named Cerys, the privileged daughter of a member of the British Parliament and his socialite wife. Even as a small child Cerys was very gifted at pencil sketching, which would occupy her for hours. From the first time she had seen a parade in which the British Army marched proudly by, she almost obsessively sketched soldiers in their handsome red-coated uniforms. It became a lighthearted family belief that Cerys must have been prescient; after completing her education at boarding school, where she tirelessly pursued her artistic talent and won several awards for her drawings, she met and then married a distinguished army officer in a spectacular wedding attended by hundreds of Britain's socially elite. Her husband was handsome, cultured, attentive, wealthy, and wildly popular, and Cerys and her parents took great pride in how well she had married.

It was a picture-perfect life for more than three years, which made it even more of a shock when scandal hit and destroyed everything. Cerys's husband, it seemed, had been paying vast amounts of money to a young man with whom he'd had a brief, illicit affair. Knowing that the affair would shatter the husband's career, image, and life in general, the young man had demanded, and received, regular extortion payments in exchange for his silence. But he had kept demanding more and more and more, and it became apparent that he wouldn't stop until Cerys's husband didn't have a penny left to his name. Finally, seeing no other way out, the husband had informed the young man "the well was dry." He would give him one final lump-sum payment, enough to purchase the luxurious flat in which the young man lived, but that would be the end of the money, and the end of any and all contact between them. The young man, enraged, headed straight to the husband's commanding officer with a handful of sexually explicit notes the husband had written to him and exposed Cerys's husband as a homosexual.

The notes had the exact effect the young man had known they would. Cerys's husband was dishonorably discharged from the army, and word of the reason why spread like wildfire through Britain's socially elite. The fact that he hanged himself days later was almost incidental to the family's public humiliation. Cerys spent the rest of her life in seclusion at their country house, bitter, betrayed, and trying to drink her pain away. She became estranged from her parents, who unfairly blamed her for their dramatic loss of status, and she died at the age of sixty-eight of liver failure.

Small wonder then that Coco Chanel was so willing to fictionalize the details and, in her mind, shameful circumstances of her childhood. She was mistrustful, seeming to be perpetually braced for betrayal, while her amazing talent propelled her to legendary status among the world of fashion's socially elite, as those were the people who had once so unceremoniously turned away from her.

RITA HAYWORTH

The tragic life of Rita Hayworth was actually the twenty-ninth incarnation of a spirit whose journeys on earth won't be completed for three more lifetimes. Her greatest challenges in her most recent life—among them, chronic mistreatment by men, alcohol addiction, and Alzheimer's disease—have plagued her over and over again, and she continues to chart them, tenacious enough to keep incarnating until she conquers them.

One of her earliest lives was in Persia in the third century. Her name was Hester, and she was an uncommonly beautiful child but was born with a withered arm. Her father, a cruelly narcissistic man, wanted her killed at birth; he was ashamed of having fathered a child with such a conspicuous flaw. Her mother, Soraya, fled with her to Soraya's uncle's home on the Persian Gulf, where she raised her with love and whatever advantages she could provide. (Soraya and Hester met again many centuries later, when Hester was Rita Hayworth and Soraya was her loving daughter, Yasmin, who cared for her throughout her years battling Alzheimer's, until the day she died.)

Hester's beauty grew as she did, and she would have had many suitors if it hadn't been for her withered arm. Due to ignorance and superstition, her birth defect was regarded as an indication of a curse, and no matter how attracted men were to her flawless face, they were unwilling to bring a cursed wife into their households.

By the time Hester was in her late teens she had grown deeply depressed, convinced that if she didn't have a husband and children in her future, she had no purpose in this world. And so the day after Soraya died of a bacterial infection, Hester took her own life, drowning herself in the Gulf waters near her uncle's home.

Rita's desire to earn male love and acceptance inspired her to chart a life for herself in Appalachia in the mid-1800s. Her name was Bonnie, and she was the only child of a poor farmer and his wife. Bonnie's mother suffered from a severe alcohol addiction, and Bonnie was born with alcohol in her system, which led to the same addiction in her later years. As a child, though, because her mother would often disappear for days at a time, Bonnie became her father's helper and essentially the woman of the house. She would work the fields, clean, cook, and even help her father with his moonshine production, which both supplemented the family income and fed her mother's alcoholism. Bonnie was too determined to be of use to her father to fall into the trap of addiction, but in a tragic act of betrayal, in her early teens her father encouraged her to prostitute herself to his regular moonshine customers. To please him, she obliged without hesitation or a single thought to the fact that she was being used rather than loved.

Bonnie was fifteen years old when her mother died of liver disease. Two months later, her father was crushed to death under the wheels of a runaway wagon. With no reason to stay where she was, Bonnie found her way, through one of her father's customers, to a job as a barmaid on a riverboat. It was there that she gave in to her dormant alcoholism and returned to prostitution—not for the money, but because Bonnie hoped that one day she would please one of her clients so much that he would fall in love with her and want to marry her. By the time she was thirty, her looks—which had always been pleasant but unremarkable—had been ravaged by too much alcohol and too many uncaring men. She began wearing a mask over her eyes in order to disguise the toll her life had taken on her, and to her surprise, the mask tended to attract men who had previously been disinterested in her. This led her to the conclusion that she was more desirable when she was in disguise.

Alcohol slowly but surely destroyed Bonnie's body and mind. When she was thirty-five, a sympathetic client finally took her under his wing, removing her and her few belongings from the riverboat, and checking her into a sanitarium in Baton Rouge. She still insisted on wearing her mask and by then had no idea who she was or where she'd come from. In her hospital gown and mask, she would compulsively pace from one end of the sanitarium to the other. Incredibly, toward the end of her life, she firmly believed that she had a withered arm, remembering her long-ago incarnation in Persia, and accused the other patients of disliking her because of it. She would occasionally introduce herself to her caretakers as Hester, which they dismissed as the delusions of a madwoman.

One day she wandered away from the sanitarium, believing she was headed for the waters of the Persian Gulf to drown herself. No one looked for her as, in her confusion, she became hopelessly lost and was unable to find her way to any place familiar to her. She died of dehydration and other complications from her already compromised health, and worse, she died alone.

She'll be back in 2026 for a life of extraordinary intellect, in which she'll be a renowned researcher in pursuit of reliable alcohol and drug addiction cures. She'll also be fiercely independent, not marrying until she's in her thirties, and then only to a man who adores her and deeply respects her for exactly who she is.

JIMI HENDRIX

Music was a constant in the thirty-nine incarnations of Jimi Hendrix. It was a vehicle that helped to elevate him above a world he frequently found to be too dark for his fragile, wandering soul. He returned to earth time and time again, determined to pierce that darkness, and when he finally succeeded, as he did this last time around by leaving a legacy of music to elevate others, he went Home to stay.

His life in twelfth-century England, for example, during the reign of King Henry II, began in north London. He was named Philippe, after his maternal grandfather, and he was the son of a popular pub owner. His mother had died during childbirth. His father, deeply grieving for the loss of his wife, took his own life. Philippe was then sent to an orphanage, where he was treated well and learned to sew. By the time he was twelve, he'd begun to make brilliantly colored clothing for himself, dyed from the roots, berries, and leaves he found in the woods near the orphanage, which he loved to explore.

When he left the orphanage at the age of fourteen to make his own way, Philippe took nothing with him but his small, colorful wardrobe and a haunting singing voice, which led quickly to his relatively successful profession: he traveled the streets of London singing the news of the day, often in the form of spontaneous, very clever poetry. Between his voice, his clothing, and his poetry, he had no trouble attracting the donations on which he lived and the occasional sponsors with whom he stayed, until his restlessness took hold of him again and he moved on.

Emotionally, he constantly fought depression. He felt a deep disillusionment about his place in this world and a nagging belief that, if he died at any given moment, no one would care beyond a passing thought. He talked frequently about being homesick. The few who knew his background assumed he was referring to the orphanage, where he still had friends, regular meals, and a reliable place to sleep. Only after he was found dead of hypothermia at the age of nineteen, hidden in a grove of trees not far from houses at which he knew he was welcome, did it become apparent that Philippe had been homesick for a place that couldn't be found on earth.

Jimi came back in eastern Europe in the 1400s as a lighthearted, adventurous boy named Emilian. The youngest of six children born to a Romanian family, he was their primary source of laughter and playfulness, and ultimately their primary source of income as well. From the age of four, Emilian loved to make up songs to amuse his family and friends, and as he grew, so did the quality and sophistication of the songs. The family formed a band and began traveling throughout Romania and Hungary in a classic gypsy wagon, dancing and performing Emilian's songs, which gained them some popularity in the area.

One day when Emilian was fourteen his older and deeply troubled brother, Boiko, burglarized a house in the Hungarian town in which the family had been performing. Despite Boiko's remorseless confession to his parents, they decided that Emilian should take the blame; they believed that, because of Emilian's youth and the force of his personality, his punishment by the townspeople would be much less severe than the consequences Boiko might face. Emilian felt completely betrayed by his family and ran away to Debrecen, Hungary. Music of any kind was thereafter a cruel reminder of that betrayal, so he never sang or wrote another song. Nor did he ever talk about his past among any new friends.

To make a living, he became an apprentice cobbler and then took over the thriving business when his elderly boss and mentor passed away. He married his mentor's granddaughter, Bianka, with whom he had two sons and a daughter, and within a few years he was enjoying great success, known throughout Debrecen and the surrounding villages as a fine craftsman and a generous, funny, reliable friend. Only a rare few saw the sadness that lay beneath the surface of his easy laughter, but no one asked about it. Emilian was a very private man; not even Bianka knew about the pain that had led him to Debrecen and to her.

When Emilian first became ill, with undiagnosed tuberculosis, he instinctively knew that his lifetime was coming to a slow, painful end. He began working day and night, compromising his health even more, to leave his wife and children a wealth of beautiful hand-made shoes and boots to sell so that they would be well provided for without him. And then, with the explanation that he was going away because he didn't want them to be put through the agony of watching him die, Emilian left his beloved family, his home, his business, and Debrecen behind. He set out in search of whomever might be left of his parents, brothers, and sisters, hoping to make peace with them before his life ended.

He found two of his sisters in the small family house in Romania, where they'd lived before their lives on the road had begun. Their mother was the only other surviving relative; she lived nearby with her second husband and his grown children. While Emilian's sisters took care of him until he died, his mother refused to see him, unable to forgive him for breaking her heart all those years earlier, without a thought as to how she'd actually broken his too.

Emilian's mother returned to be Jimi's mother in his last incarnation, in the ill-fated hope that the two of them could finally forge a relationship that would bring them both more joy than pain. Jimi Hendrix's brilliant musical gifts and his tireless traveling also came naturally to him from centuries of experience. And who better to embrace rainbows as a continuing theme throughout his amazing career than a man who once learned to dye his clothing with plants and trees that had brightened his life in a British orphanage?

BETTY FORD

The remarkable woman we knew as Betty Ford, former First Lady of the United States and founder of the Betty Ford Center for alcohol and drug abuse rehabilitation, completed her thirty-ninth and final incarnation on July 8, 2011. Some of the qualities for which she was best known—overcoming obstacles, helping others to overcome those same obstacles, and unapologetically maintaining her own strong identity while married to a powerful man—were qualities that had taken root in her soul several lifetimes ago.

She was called Valentina in eighteenth-century Russia, and was the oldest of three children born to an abusive bully of a father, who made and sold black-market vodka. Valentina's mother was a timid, dependent woman, too afraid of her husband to protect the children from his abuse. Theirs was an oppressive, joyless household. From the time the children were very small, their mother, at their father's insistence, gave them sips of vodka to calm them down or make them sleep, while their mother drank to "calm her nerves." Ironically, the only sober person in the family was the father, who saw alcohol as a way to make an enormous amount of illegal money and to exhibit weakness that he could exploit in those who abused it. He wasn't about to relinquish his sense of superiority over his wife, children, and customers by indulging in his own product.

Valentina was left to her own devices to find what joy this world had to offer. She found that joy in her passion for reading and in her extraordinary gift for ballet, which was discovered quite by accident. At the age of five, on a trip to the doctor with her mother, she had stopped to look in the window of a storefront, where a ballet class was in progress. Enthralled, Valentina began duplicating the movements she was watching and doing it with such remarkable grace and accuracy that the instructor came outside to meet her and invite her to join the class. To her and her mother's surprise, her father approved of the classes—not because he was interested in what Valentina wanted but because he knew that a truly gifted ballerina might someday bring a lot of money into the household.

Valentina was indeed a gifted ballerina, and by the time she was in her mid-teens she had become a featured performer in the Bolshoi Ballet. She had also become as addicted to alcohol as her mother and her two brothers were, but her brilliant talent, discipline, and determination kept the addiction from interfering with her performances. At her father's insistence, she gave him what he believed was her entire salary every month. He had no idea that she was setting aside some money for a "rainy day," which came along less than a year after she'd joined the Bolshoi.

She arrived home one night to find that her father had severely beaten her eight-year-old brother and badly injured her ten-year-old brother when he had tried to intervene. Her mother had hid, sobbing, in a toolshed. Her father had then fled the house, as he often did for days at a time, intending to further punish them by depriving them of the money needed to buy food. Valentina quickly packed up her mother and brothers before he returned and, with the help of her own funds and a friend in the Bolshoi with connections throughout Europe, they fled to France and eventually England, to start a new life.

They settled temporarily into the maids' quarters of the home of her friend's relatives. Valentina, thanks to her reputation with the Bolshoi, quickly established herself in England as a popular, gifted classical dance teacher and was able to afford a small flat for herself and her mother and brothers. But her mother and her two brothers were showing disturbing signs of alcohol addiction, which made Valentina take a long hard look at herself and realize that she was addicted too. She could hardly expect them to overcome their addictions without her own willingness to set an example, so with great difficulty she managed to break the daily alcohol habit to which she and her brothers had become accustomed since childhood. Not only was she able to inspire her family to become clean and sober, but she could also tell them what to expect along the way and help them through the hardest parts. Her brothers succeeded. Her mother didn't and died of liver failure, along with a general loss of her will to live, two years after they had arrived in England.

Through the mother of one of her ballet students, Valentina was introduced to a widowed member of the British aristocracy. They were married within months of meeting, and Valentina and her brothers moved into his country estate. At her insistence, not her husband's, she continued teaching and single-handedly put her brothers through school, believing it was her responsibility, not his, and wanting it to be perfectly clear that she had married for love and not for money. One brother became a highly respected teacher of earth sciences while the other became a successful attorney.

Valentina became pregnant but suffered a miscarriage, which devastated both her and her husband. But rather than bringing the couple closer together, their mutual grief created more distance between them than the marriage could bear, and they separated amicably after six years together. She moved back to the flat she'd previously shared with her mother and brothers and went right on teaching at her thriving ballet school. Her ex-husband, out of fondness for her, and despite her appreciative objections, bought the flat for her and paid her monthly expenses. As one of her ways of sharing her good fortune, she recruited several talented students whose parents couldn't afford dance lessons, and she taught them free of charge.

Valentina was forty-eight when she fell in her flat and, in the process, knocked herself unconscious and pierced her breast with a letter opener she had been holding. Her brothers found her two days later. She went Home in contented peace about the life she'd lived, and her courage, strength, independence, and kindness continued to inspire everyone who'd known her.

Cell memory may have manifested itself in her tendency toward addiction and in a wounded breast, which later translated to breast cancer, but it also contributed to her talent for dance and other qualities that inspired and saved the lives of whole new generations who knew her as Betty Ford. And it's worth mentioning that the younger of her two brothers in her incarnation as

Valentina was with her again in her last life as her son, Steven.

STEVE MCQUEEN

The superstar actor, racecar driver, and motorcycle rider we knew as Steve McQueen left his forty-eighth incarnation in 1980 and will be back twice more before he considers the earthly part of his soul's journey complete. By all accounts, toward the end of his life McQueen had become an evangelical Christian, and the first of his two remaining lifetimes will be spent as a missionary, to be born in Nevada in 2025 and to devote himself to bringing the word of Christ to the most poverty-stricken areas of Asia, Africa, and South America. In a way, that incarnation will bring him full circle with one of his earlier ones in twelfth-century Europe, when he was one of the Knights of the Temple of Solomon, better known as the Knights Templar.

The Knights Templar were initially founded after the First Crusade for the purpose of protecting pilgrims as they traveled to Jerusalem and other sites considered sacred in the Christian religion. They were incredibly effective fundraisers, once they were sanctioned by the church, and seemingly more worthy of trust because they had taken vows of poverty. The Templars were also the most fearless, well-equipped, and well-trained fighters of their day. Steve McQueen, then known as Gerard (although not the Templars' Grand Master, Gerard de Ridefort), was one of the Templars' fiercest warriors and a brilliant battle tactician.

Gerard's commitment to the Templars was as soul-deep as his commitment to God and Christ, so when King Philip IV of France, who was deeply in debt to the Templars, ordered them to be arrested and tortured into confessing that they'd committed heresy as part of their initiation, Gerard was one of the few who refused. He died of his wounds from that torture, fulfilling his belief that the greatest honor a Templar could achieve was to die a martyr.

McQueen's subsequent incarnations reflected an internal struggle between his deep faith in Christianity and his fearless willingness to do whatever was needed for what he perceived to be a worthy cause. If what was needed happened to be against the law, his warrior energy from his life as a Templar propelled him for the sake of that worthy cause. And after being tortured to death for crimes he hadn't committed, by the agents of a king who simply didn't want to repay a debt, "the law" had become a gray area for him.

In the mid-1800s, he was born in the woods of South Carolina to a fifteen-year-old girl and a

forty-two-year-old handyman who made the majority of his meager living cutting down trees and selling the resulting firewood. His name was Robert, and
when he was two years old his mother decided that
she was too young to deal with the responsibilities of
having a child. She left Robert in the dubious care of
his father in a lean-to ten miles from the nearest town.
Robert's father did the best he could, but he was painfully aware that his best wasn't nearly good enough,
so when Robert was four, he was taken to his aunt's
house in town to be raised, a house that happened to
be a brothel.

Robert wasn't exactly sure what went on inside the
rooms of the run-down house, but he caught on quickly
that the more often men came and went, the happier his
aunt and the other women who lived there seemed to
be and the more food appeared on the table. He began
putting on performances in front of the house to draw
in the male passersby, singing, dancing, and making up
rhymes at the top of his lungs, delighting both the residents of the house and the neighborhood in general, and
even the occasional policemen who stopped by looking
grim but left smiling an hour or two later. Every few
months his father would visit, bringing a little money
for the care of his son, which made a bigger impression
on Robert than he was aware of at the time.

He tried going to school, but he was relentlessly teased for his poor hygiene and the inevitable holes in his clothing and got into a lot of playground fights, so he stopped attending after several weeks. Determined to fill his days with something worthwhile and to supplement the household income with a few extra pennies, Robert's aunt prevailed upon a frequent customer of hers, a local clockmaker and locksmith who was known to hire young boys to run errands, make deliveries, and clean up around the shop. Unbeknownst to Robert's aunt, the man was essentially patterning his life after the character Fagin in *Oliver Twist*—Robert and the other boys, once their boss was satisfied that they were bright and could be trusted, were trained to use locksmithing tools to break into the wealthier homes in town and return with whatever valuables they could quickly and easily steal. Those items were then sold at markets in neighboring towns. Robert—small, fearless, and an incredibly fast runner—became one of his boss's most valued young employees, and gained his boss's praise and his aunt's gratitude for the extra income, which more than made up for any guilt Robert might have felt about the thefts he was committing. He also learned to love the rush of adrenaline he felt, and he might have continued a life of crime if, when he was fourteen, he hadn't been caught by an enraged wealthy homeowner and subsequently handed over to the police.

His boss put on an impressive display of shock and horror at what his young employee had been up to. His aunt, not wanting to jeopardize her tenuous relationship with local law enforcement, wanted nothing to do with him. It was Robert's father who arrived in tears to free his son. He handed over every dime he had, including what little he'd set aside for food, to pay the fine. Robert was deeply moved at the sacrifice his father had made on his behalf, and heartbroken to have disappointed him. He returned to his father's lean-to with him, to help him with his odd jobs and woodcutting and to see to it that his father always had enough to eat.

They became very close, especially after Robert's father apologized for having left his son on the doorstep of a brothel. Robert forgave him, genuinely understanding that his father could barely afford to take care of himself, plus had had no idea how to provide for a child. Robert, young and strong and tireless as he was, stayed with his father and slowly took over his business as his father's health declined. Robert's father died of consumption, now called tuberculosis, eight years later. Robert took care of him as best he could and never left his side. It only took Robert another year to succumb to tuberculosis as well, but he went Home at peace, knowing that when he'd arrived at a crossroads, he'd chosen the path that had led him to loving and being loved for the first and only time in his life.

Two people from that incarnation accompanied Steve McQueen into his most recent lifetime. One was his father, who returned as his great-uncle, Claude, on whose farm McQueen happily spent much of his childhood and under whose influence he thrived. The other was his mother, who returned as his mother again, abandoning him and reclaiming him several times, more disruptive than nurturing but answering a question Robert had privately asked himself over and over again almost a hundred years earlier: "What would have happened if my mother had ever come back?" (For the record, Steve McQueen's mother, Julia, has another eight lifetimes ahead before she will finally get it right.)

GRACE KELLY

One of the earliest and certainly the most influential of Grace Kelly's thirty-four incarnations took place on the Somali peninsula in the mid-thirteenth century. She was named Jwahir, and she was one of three daughters born to a successful camel trader and his wife. Since the birth of Jwahir's younger sister, her mother had been chronically ill with what we would now call chronic fatigue syndrome, which left her unable to care for her children and the household. Jwahir took on those duties by the time she was ten, without a word of complaint. She was devoted to her parents and sisters and especially close to her father, whose tireless work ethic and loyalty to his family she greatly admired.

Jwahir was twelve when her father fell from a loft in his camel stables and injured his back. He was incapacitated and in severe pain, and in her eagerness to help, Jwahir began treating him with long healing massages and herbal remedies from their garden. Against all odds, her father was soon able to walk and function again. Within weeks he'd fully recovered. His many buyers were amazed at the speed with which he had returned to health, and he proudly told them about the "magic" his daughter had performed to make him well. Those buyers were impressed enough to tell the amazing recovery story on their many travels, so before long word had spread far and wide about the young girl whose herbs and touch were blessed with the power to heal.

Jwahir and Ayan, the eldest and youngest of the three sisters, were inseparable, and Ayan also became an invaluable helper with both the housekeeping chores and the prodigious herb garden as people began traveling from as far away as Kenya to be healed by Jwahir. Jwahir could have turned her gifts into a very lucrative business, but she refused to accept compensation, believing her healing powers would be rescinded if she exploited them or took credit for them in any way. It also confused her and weighed heavily on her heart that with all her success at helping total strangers, she was unable to heal her ailing mother, and for reasons she never understood. She had a very deep spiritual core and spent her first and last waking hours of every day in prayer, always including pleas for her mother's health in her long conversations with God.

Jwahir was also remarkably psychic. She awoke one night from a sound sleep and ran to her sister's bed because she "knew" Ayan was in trouble. Ayan, an infant at the time, was choking on a toy and would have died if Jwahir hadn't arrived exactly when she did to pull the toy out of Ayan's throat. Jwahir could also accurately alert her father days ahead of time as to when a new buyer would be coming to look at his healthy, well-fed, well-trained camels and whether or not the new buyer's arrival would result in a sale.

What was most unusual about Jwahir's psychic gift, though, was her absolute certainty that one day she would be a much-admired princess. She assumed it was a glimpse into her adulthood in the lifetime she was living then. She couldn't imagine how marriage to a prince could happen to such a modest, simple girl who didn't even aspire to a life far away from her parents and sisters. She had no idea that she was having the very rare experience of seeing several incarnations into her own future.

When Jwahir's father died, she took over the family business, continued with her healing practice, and married one of her father's most trusted employees, who dealt directly with other camel traders and prospective buyers. The older of her sisters had long since left home by then, but Ayan stayed by Jwahir's side, even after their mother passed away. The two sisters had learned from their father to be smart, honest businesswomen, and they used a large percentage of their profits to both feed needy families in the area and build a modest healing and worship center, which was also open to those who needed food and shelter.

Jwahir and Ayan both died in a fire that destroyed the family home, when Jwahir was forty-one and Ayan had just turned thirty-four. They met again centuries later, by mutual design, when Jwahir returned to earth as Grace Kelly and Ayan returned as Grace's daughter, Stephanie.

Grace Kelly will be back for one more incarnation, having learned from her life of wealth, privilege, and acclaim that, while her charitable work as the Princess of Monaco had been enormously fulfilling, she had lost sight of the deep, sustaining spiritual core that her spirit mind remembered and yearned for.

Her next and last incarnation will be a privileged one as well. She'll be born on the big island of Hawaii in 2023 to an insanely successful clothing designer and her husband. She'll be given every opportunity to become a shallow, self-centered, unproductive woman, but instead she'll be a hardworking, well-known architect, appreciative of the advantages her family provided but too bright, talented, and independent not to insist on her own achievements. Her great challenge in that life will be to find and live in a balance between material wealth and the far more essential wealth that comes from exploring and making good humanitarian use of the highly advanced soul God created her to become.

STEVE JOBS

It won't surprise you any more than it surprised me that Steven Paul Jobs was and is an extraordinary spirit. He's only incarnated once before. He carefully calculated the timing of his second incarnation to maximize his impact on this world, and he won't be back for another lifetime on earth. He's already hard at work again on the Other Side, infusing the results of his research and experiments—in this case, revolutionizing space travel as historically as he revolutionized the relationship between humankind and computers—to be actualized by some of the greatest minds here on earth. Thanks in large part to Steve Jobs's continuing efforts at Home, manned intergalactic travel will be a reality by the year 2052.

In his first incarnation, he was born in Pisa, Italy, in 1564, the oldest of six children born to a renowned musician and his wife. His name was Galileo. When he was eight years old, the family moved to Florence, his father's birthplace. He was sent to a Camaldolese monastery to be educated, and he loved the strict, solitary life he found there. He intended to join the Order, against the wishes of his father, who hoped his eldest son would study medicine instead. His father's wishes won out, and Galileo ended up pursuing a medical degree at the University of Pisa, returning to Florence only during summer to pursue his real loves, mathematics and science. Ultimately, even his father couldn't overlook his son's disinterest in medicine, and Galileo left the university without finishing enough courses to earn his degree.

He began teaching mathematics and, in 1586, wrote his first scientific book, *The Little Balance*, about a hydrostatic balance he'd invented. A year later he traveled to Rome to meet Clavius, a mathematics professor at the Jesuit college there. Galileo failed to achieve the appointment to teach mathematics at the University of Bologna he had been hoping for, but he did impress Clavius with the results of experiments he'd been performing regarding centers of gravity, and the two men became longtime correspondents.

At about this same time Galileo became fascinated by and an instructor in the fine arts, particularly in the techniques of perspective and chiaroscuro, the artistic traditions of Florence, and the paintings of the great Renaissance artists. This added an aesthetic sensibility to his mathematical scientific mind. Over the next several years he also taught and lectured on the subjects of geometry, mechanics, and astronomy at the University of Padua and made several important scientific discoveries, including a substantial improvement on the telescope. Through his improved telescope, he made remarkable discoveries he described in a book called *Starry Messenger*, which became very famous in its day.

While Galileo was in Padua he met and began a relationship with a Venetian woman named Marina Gamba. Despite the fact that he was still a devout

Roman Catholic, he never married her, but they did have three children together.

It was a popular belief among astronomers at the time that everything in our solar system, except the earth and the moon, orbited around the sun, and that the sun orbited the stationary planet earth. Galileo, on the other hand, ultimately agreed with Copernicus, a well-known mathematician and astronomer from the sixteenth century who had proposed instead that the earth and the other planets orbited the sun. To some powerful Roman Catholics, this was contrary to facts about the physical world described in the Holy Scripture. Galileo finally, and respectfully, wrote a book called *Dialogue Concerning the Two Chief World Systems—Ptolemaic and Copernican,* defending the Copernican theory. It was a book that took him six years to write because of his failing health and was published in 1632. In response, the Catholic Church's Inquisition summoned him to be tried in Rome in 1633 on suspicion of heresy. He was found guilty and ordered to denounce the Copernican theory and to remain under house arrest for the rest of his life. Not only was his book banned, but all his works, including any future books, were also banned.

Galileo was allowed to live under house arrest at his villa near Florence, where he was guarded twenty-four hours a day by officers from the Inquisition. During the first year there he was shattered by the news that his eldest child, his daughter Virginia, who'd been loyally and lovingly supportive of her father, had died. His grief prevented him from working for several months, but eventually he undertook and completed *Discourses and Mathematical Demonstrations Concerning Two New Sciences*. By order of the Inquisition this book could not be published in Italy, so it was eventually smuggled out of Italy and instead published in Holland in 1638. To this day, Galileo is commonly referred to as the father of modern physics, due in no small part to the high praise this book received from Albert Einstein more than two centuries later.

The same year *Discourses* was published, Galileo went blind. He also suffered terribly from a hernia and from insomnia, and he was eventually allowed to seek help from doctors in Florence. By 1642, his health was further compromised by recurring fevers and heart palpitations, and on January 8, 1642, he died at the age of seventy-seven.

In later centuries the Catholic Church authorized the publication of his complete scientific works, referred to him as a hero, expressing regret at the way he'd been treated, and acknowledging his profound contributions to astronomy, physics, mathematics, and modern science. After an initial unceremonious burial, due to his condemnation by the Church, a monument was erected in the main body of the Basilica of Santa Croce in Florence and he was reburied there in 1737.

Galileo made an incalculable impact on this world in the late 1500s and early 1600s. He made every bit as much of an impact in the fifty-six years he spent in his second and last incarnation, which lasted from 1955 to 2011, when his name was Steve Jobs.

JANE RUSSELL

Of Jane Russell's thirty-nine incarnations, with one more left to go on this earth to complete her soul's journey, two in particular directed her toward her lifetime as the celebrated actress who returned Home to the Other Side on February 28, 2011.

The first of those lives was in ancient Egypt. Her name was Sekhmet, and she was the only child of a soldier who went on to become a high officer in the court of the fascinating and powerful Queen Hatshepsut. Hatshepsut, wife of King Thutmose II, declared herself pharaoh when Thutmose died. Presumably to make herself more acceptable to the Egyptian people, who had rarely experienced a female pharaoh, Hatshepsut dressed as a man throughout her reign, including wearing a false beard and the royal robes of a king, and Egypt flourished under her command.

Sekhmet was an uncommonly beautiful and bright child. She easily caught the eye of Hatshepsut on visits to the temple and then impressed her with her loyalty and discretion, qualities she'd learned from her highly respected father. She was a gifted student of both mathematics and astrology, and also of human nature. In her early teens, she instinctively recognized that Hatshepsut, despite being constantly surrounded by servants and sycophants, was lonely and in need of a trustworthy confidant. The unconventional pharaoh gradually looked to Sekhmet to fill that role, and Sekhmet never betrayed her confidences, not even to her own father, who worked closely with Hatshepsut until his death when Sekhmet was twenty-one. Sekhmet's loyalty was rewarded with a life of luxury. She was comfortable with her public invisibility and had taken very much to heart her father's lesson that there is a great advantage in fulfilling the needs and keeping the secrets of someone in power—in this case, someone of whom Sekhmet was genuinely fond.

When Thutmose III, Hatshepsut's nephew, succeeded her to the throne of Egypt, he had both Hatshepsut and Sekhmet briefly imprisoned, according to my Spirit Guide, Francine. He destroyed many of the temples built during his aunt's reign, in order to protect the historical illusion of an all-male lineage of pharaohs. Sekhmet managed to escape and lived the rest of her life simply and reclusively until she died at the age of forty-two of an infection caused by an abscessed tooth.

The next incarnation that had a major impact on the journey of Jane Russell's soul began with her birth in Pienza, Italy, in the late 1500s. Octavia, as she was known then, was the fifth child of a desperately poor couple who couldn't afford to feed themselves. Like her older sisters and brother before her, Octavia was abandoned on the streets of Pienza at the age of four. She never spoke or uttered a single sound except to earn the spare change of passersby with her angelic renditions of hymns. She had listened to and memorized these hymns in reverent silence outside the open cathedral windows of the Pienza Duomo.

The tiny homeless child and her haunting voice eventually attracted the attention of a modest, loving family named Santos. They welcomed her into their home and raised her with their son, Gianni, who was ten years older than Octavia. Gianni adored her and enjoyed teaching her, playing games with her, and taking her to mass every week at the Duomo, where as a lost child Octavia had been too shy and had felt too undeserving to enter. Gianni, in fact, was the only person to whom Octavia ever spoke, and she only did so on rare occasions and only in whispers, never in complete sentences.

When she was eight years old, Octavia's health, already compromised from the neglect and malnourishment she'd suffered during her early childhood, couldn't withstand a tuberculosis plague that swept through the hills of Tuscany, and she passed to the Other Side surrounded by her kind, adoptive parents and her adoring, devoted stepbrother. (It's worth mentioning that Octavia and Gianni met again many incarnations later, when they were known as Jane Russell and Howard Hughes.)

Jane Russell entered her most recent lifetime with fears of being poor and being abandoned. These two previous lifetimes, in particular, had led her to believe that safety, security, and love were rewards limited only to those who were exceptionally beautiful or exceptionally gifted. In her most recent life, of course, she chose to be both.

One of the most fabled stories of her career was Howard Hughes's "discovery" of her for his movie *The Outlaw.* The truth is, Howard Hughes didn't discover Jane Russell; he *recognized* her, as surely as she recognized him, from their cherished closeness all those centuries ago, and just as they'd both charted for themselves before they had begun the most famous of their incarnations.

During a successful career, which spanned forty years, Jane Russell was married to two public figures—a football star and an actor. But as her lifetime progressed, she found herself yearning for less prominence and more privacy. She and her third husband, a realtor, moved to Sedona, Arizona. Finally having satisfied her soul's yearning for safety, security, and love, she was able to focus on developing the inner beauty and spiritual wisdom she'd always had in abundance but had rarely explored during her lives on earth. And there, within her, she found peace and the ultimate love of God, where no greater safety and security exists.

In her next and final incarnation, beginning in 2016, Jane Russell will be a grocer in a small town on the Maine coast, married to a commercial fisherman, remarkably unremarkable, quietly spiritual, devoted to God, tirelessly active in a charity for neglected and abandoned children, and above all, the happiest she's ever been.

WINSTON CHURCHILL

The historic world leader Winston Churchill finished his fifty-first and final incarnation on January 24, 1965. Each of his incarnations, even the ones in which he was just a simple, ordinary man, was a building block toward the depth, courage, and integrity of a Nobel Prize–winning author and a brilliant statesman instrumental in ending World War II.

His outstanding intellect is no surprise when you know of his life in Greece during the time of Aristotle. His name was Plotinus, and he was a philosopher, writer, and teacher who dreamed of a culture that was good, fair, and harmonious. He was known for his personal integrity and was highly regarded, even by those who didn't agree with his philosophies. He also had an innate gift for the art of diplomacy, which he brought with him through cell memory into every lifetime he lived. He never married in his life as Plotinus; nor did he father any children, although his character was so exemplary that he was entrusted with many of his colleagues' children for their guidance and education. He lived to be sixty-six in that life and died of a long illness, which severely compromised his body and mind, not at all unlike the series of strokes that took the life of Churchill many incarnations later.

Later, in the 1800s, came a lifetime as a barrister in England. He was named Lucien, after his French father, and he was a childhood friend of Prince Albert, the great love of Queen Victoria's life. His genius as a litigator was widely renowned, but Lucien fiercely protected his privacy and his relative anonymity, gearing his practice toward pro bono work and legally protecting the rights of the underprivileged.

He was first and foremost a family man, with a wife named Margaret (who returned with him as his wife, Clementine, in his incarnation as Winston Churchill) and three daughters he adored. He had a wide variety of talents, which he modestly preferred to call interests, most of which he had developed strictly for the enjoyment of his daughters. His gifts as a writer and artist, for example, were expressed through writing and illustrating countless unpublished children's books for them about a little girl named Henriette, who was born with only one eye but who, despite her supposed "imperfection," had wonderful adventures with forest animals as a child and grew into a successful dressmaker for all the royal families of Europe. The stories particularly inspired Lucien's youngest daughter, Marie, challenged since birth with a disfigured right foot that resulted in a severe limp. That Henriette happened to resemble Marie and share Marie's love of animals was no coincidence.

Through his childhood friend, Albert, Lucien gained the respect and fondness of Queen Victoria, although Lucien never exploited that relationship or used it to elevate his stature in British society. He did become one of her closest confidants during her intense grief when Prince Albert died, since he'd known Albert so well and understood the depth of her loss more than most. To show her appreciation, the queen offered Lucien and his family one of her country houses, but he respectfully declined the offer, preferring to stay in the comfortable but unremarkable home in which he and Margaret had enjoyed their happy marriage and raised their much beloved children.

Lucien lived until his forty-fifth birthday in that lifetime and died in a way that exemplified his fearlessness and willingness to lay down his life for a just cause. He was visiting his oldest daughter at her millinery shop in London when the deranged husband of one of the shop's clients burst in with a pistol, accusing Lucien's daughter of stealing his wife's money. The man took aim, but an instant before he pulled the trigger, Lucien, without hesitation and looking the gunman straight in the eye, stepped in to shield his daughter and took the bullet that was intended for her. He died instantly and without a moment of regret about his life or death.

It was only ten short years later when he chose to incarnate again as Winston Churchill. It's rare for spirits to return from Home so quickly, but he knew he was needed on earth, and he knew the incarnation had arrived that he'd been preparing for since his soul was created.

AMY WINEHOUSE

Amy Winehouse's spirit is very advanced, which often means a series of difficult lifetimes have been charted in which lessons must be learned the hard way. In Amy's case, one of the lessons she's struggled to learn in her forty-two incarnations is that she is indeed worthy of the best life has to offer. Another is that punishment, whether from outside influences or from herself, isn't an inevitable price of success. She'll be back twice more to complete her education on earth.

One of the lifetimes that set the stage for her struggle with self-worth was in Haiti in the late 1500s. Her name was Matias, and she was one of six children born to a homeless, dirt-poor couple who'd figured out that they could make money by selling their offspring to the handful of wealthy landowners on the island. Matias was sold to a rich family who owned a sugar plantation. She was trained to be the personal maid to the family's eldest daughter, a vain, cruel, spoiled girl who enjoyed asserting her alleged superiority by falsely accusing Matias of everything from theft to assault, knowing that Matias would be punished with severe beatings.

A light at the end of the tunnel appeared when Matias met and fell in love with one of the family's slaves, a smart, hardworking young man named Claude. He'd been as abused and mistreated as Matias and vowed to run away with her to start a new life together as soon as he found a way to support the two of them and the children they dreamed of having.

Claude was in the process of keeping that promise, securing a job as a shipbuilder through a complex series of connections among the family's other employees. Unfortunately, a few of those employees had learned that they could gain favor with the family by passing along news of any trouble or disloyalty among the workers. So, before Matias and Claude could finalize their escape plans, the plantation owner found out what they were up to and had them both quietly and discreetly executed.

An incarnation in Hawaii in the early 1800s seemed, at first glance, to be a well-deserved contrast to her tortured life in Haiti. Her name was Haku then, and she was a small, pretty girl with delicate features and an uncommonly sweet singing voice, which she was too shy to let anyone hear. She was an only child, born to a stonemason and his wife, who'd come to believe that they would never be blessed with children. They regarded Haku as a miracle and cherished her. They wanted nothing but the best for her and gave her every advantage they could afford.

Afraid that her profound shyness might prevent her from attracting a desirable husband, her parents arranged a marriage for her with a much older, widowed businessman. Haku wasn't in love with her husband, but she admired his kindness and generosity, and he treated her very well. They shared a passion for helping the disadvantaged, and when they discovered that Haku was barren, they built a family by adopting six children from a local orphanage and prepared to give them wonderful lives.

They were ready and eager to adopt more, but an overzealous group of Catholic missionaries intervened and blocked all further adoptions until Haku and her husband vowed to convert to Catholicism and raise their children as Catholics. Shy as she was, Haku was fierce when it came to loving and protecting her children, and she felt that the missionaries were intruding on a family to whom they'd offered no help and with whom they hadn't earned the right to interfere. Her Jewish husband agreed with Haku on this, and they made arrangements to move away and live with relatives of his—ironically in Italy, a decidedly Catholic country. As sad as it made her to leave her parents in Hawaii, Haku knew the move was the best thing for her family. While they were able to live quietly and with no interference as a Jewish family in Italy, it broke

Haku's heart that her parents died before she was able to see them again.

When she returned in 1983 for her incarnation as Amy Winehouse, she charted a life for herself in which she could begin overcoming her understandable cell-memory sense of dread when good things happened. From her life in Hawaii, she brought her amazing singing voice and her father, who agreed to come back with her to protect her as best he could while also allowing her to fulfill the chart she'd written for herself. The irony, of course, is that the more successful and famous she became, the more frightened and constantly braced for disaster she felt. She began self-medicating, to numb the dread that prevented her from learning to relax and enjoy her well-earned celebrity.

She'll be back in 2019 to try again, and she's hard at work on the Other Side preparing for that next incarnation. It should be comforting for her family, friends, and fans to know that the moment she got Home, she gave a spectacular concert, now joyful, healthy, happy, and at peace.

JOAN CRAWFORD

Joan Crawford's most recent incarnation was her twenty-eighth, and she'll be back four more times to overcome the anger and rigidity that plagued her life after life after life. In fact, she's already charted her next lifetime, which will be spent in poverty on the plains of Kenya in her effort to essentially start from scratch and begin to heal her soul.

Her name was once Astrid. She was born in Austria in the sixteenth century, the only child of a popular, wildly flamboyant sculptor and his much younger wife, who'd been one of his models. Astrid's mother was a vain, entitled woman whose plans for life included social climbing, lots of travel, an endless array of glittering parties, and a long line of wealthy suitors vying for her attention. They most certainly did not include an early pregnancy and a resigned marriage to the baby's father, from whom she would have quickly moved on if he hadn't impregnated her.

Astrid, then, was already resented before she was born. The fact that she was born an uncommonly beautiful girl only compounded the problem. A boy would not have ignited the instinctive sense of competition Astrid's mother felt toward her daughter, especially when, from the moment her father first saw her, Astrid became the adored center of his world. Rather than being grateful to have such an attentive, involved father for her child, Astrid's mother sulked and raged and became abusive to both her husband and her baby, apparently believing that negative attention was better than no attention at all. She left countless emotional scars on her child before she abandoned her family when Astrid was six years old.

A more emotionally fragile little girl or a husband in love with his wife, might have been heartbroken at such abandonment; instead, neither Astrid nor her father felt anything but relief that this cruel, histrionic woman was out of their lives. The two of them lived quite happily without her. Astrid became her father's favorite model, companion, and dance partner at art shows and social events, and he became her best friend, teacher, playmate, and protector. By her mid-teens, Astrid was a beautiful, smart, sophisticated young woman with an impressive knowledge of the inner workings of the art world. She evolved naturally into a career as a very skilled art dealer for her father and other local artists.

When her father died suddenly of an aneurism at the age of fifty, Astrid had no idea how to navigate a life of her own. She quickly married one of her clients, a widower and watercolorist of her father's approximate age. They lived in his fieldstone chalet in the mountains with his fifteen-year-old stepdaughter, who was pursuing an art career herself. Her new husband was very attentive and solicitous, and his stepdaughter seemed very welcoming as well. Astrid, accustomed to being the woman of the house, did a brilliant job of pulling the somewhat neglected household into shape and keeping it that way, and with her new stepdaughter being so sweetly obedient and respectful, the newly formed family got along perfectly. Astrid successfully sold her husband's paintings and even a few of her stepdaughter's pieces while maintaining an ideal home. That she and her husband rarely spent a moment alone without the stepdaughter didn't bother her that much. She thought he was a fine man and a wonderful artist, and she couldn't imagine what she would have done if he hadn't come along to essentially provide her with a life in the wake of her father's death. She wasn't in love, but she was admired and secure, which was far more satisfying than being in love, as far as she was concerned.

It all vanished one day when Astrid returned home much earlier than expected and, to her horror, found her husband in bed with his stepdaughter. Irrationally, Astrid's immediate impulse was not to attack her husband but to attack the underage girl. A sense of betrayal consumed her, and if her husband hadn't intervened, she would undoubtedly have killed the girl. As it was, she stabbed her stepdaughter once, a wound from which the girl eventually recovered. Astrid was then committed by her husband to a women's asylum in Switzerland, where the emphasis had nothing to do with help and

rehabilitation and everything to do with simply controlling and confining. It was an unspeakably cruel
facility. It did nothing to enhance Astrid's opinion of
women or, for that matter, her fragile psyche. She went
insane and, at the age of thirty-five, committed suicide
in her tiny, locked room.

For Joan Crawford, the point of entry—the incarnation during which a wound was inflicted, which then
continues to cause subconscious pain until it's exposed
and given a chance to heal—was undoubtedly this past
life in Austria. The high value she placed on male
attention and approval as well as her notorious, instinctive mistrust of females of any age were ingrained in
her hundreds of years ago, with the added subliminal
message that women weren't to be trusted, whether
they were as overtly cruel to her as her mother and the
asylum wardens had been or as overtly sweet as her
husband's stepdaughter. Her toughness and quickness
to anger are much more understandable, in the context
of that lifetime, and what a brilliant choice on her part
to chart a life for herself this most recent time around in
which she could channel so much heightened emotion
into an acting career, where it would be put to good use
and make her such a legendary star.

None of the key players in Joan Crawford's long-
ago lifetime in Austria reappeared in this most recent

reincarnation. However, she's already charted that, after she returns for her life in Kenya, she and the Austrian mother who so resented and then abandoned her will come back as sisters and finally make peace with each other, as Joan makes her way to her spirit's greatest, most serene potential.

BOB HOPE

One of the earliest of Bob Hope's fifty-six lives was in eighteenth-century Russia, and it was a lifetime that helped establish the extraordinary work ethic that drove him in every subsequent incarnation.

His name was Alexei, and he was born to a middle-class family in Moscow. His father was a butcher who also, one day a week, sold homegrown vegetables from a horse-drawn cart. Alexei loved accompanying his father through the city streets and helping attract customers with songs, dances, and jokes. He was a very outgoing child. As the saying goes, he never met a stranger, and his father considered him to be an essential element of his modest success. Out of pride and gratitude, Alexei's father surprised his son with enough money to attend school, and through a lot of talent and intensive study, Alexei became a doctor before his father's tuition money ran out. He traveled throughout

Russia and his mother's home country of Poland, proving to be a skilled, compassionate physician whose bedside manner was filled with warmth and humor. He loved to read to his bedridden patients, playing out the roles of the characters in the books, and it was thought that the laughter and entertainment he provided were every bit as effective as his medical treatments.

His wife, Anna, traveled with him, as his helper. She eventually bore Alexei ten children, four of whom went on to become doctors too. He continued practicing medicine well into his seventies and lived to be an amazing ninety-three years old, when he died of an aneurism.

Another of Bob Hope's most significant incarnations was in Illinois in the 1800s. His name was Edgar, and he was a high-ranking colonel in the Union army during the American Civil War. He was known as a shrewd battle strategist, but he was also a fearless soldier, fighting on the front lines rather than letting his rank and renown as a strategist keep him a safe distance away. He had the respect of President Lincoln, to whom he reported on a regular basis, and his devotion to the president was unwavering and absolute. He often said that the most devastating event of his life was the assassination of President Lincoln. It was with both pride and personal rage that he was among those who helped lead the authorities to the Virginia barn where Lincoln's assassin, John Wilkes Booth, had been hiding.

Edgar never married, but he had a female companion for thirty years. Her name was Elsie, and her father was an army lieutenant, also from Illinois. Elsie was a notoriously difficult, high-strung woman—probably bipolar—and very materialistic. Edgar fell in love with her when they were both in their teens, and his extraordinary patience with her came to him naturally; his mother, who had died when he was ten, had had a history of mental illness as well, which helped him to understand and sympathize with Elsie rather than judge her. Elsie had always been very close to her father, finding him easy to manipulate with her tears and tantrums, but he was her only ally in the family. Her mother and two brothers, whom she treated terribly no matter how kind they were to her, had long since given up on her by the time her father was killed in battle.

The fact that her family had rejected her only increased Edgar's determination to take care of her and be the one person in her life who she could count on after her father had died. He built her a lovely house on the shore of a lake in Illinois, tried repeatedly but unsuccessfully to make peace between her and her estranged family, and, at her request, converted to Catholicism, which he came to embrace wholeheartedly.

Late one night, when Edgar was forty-eight, he and Elsie were home alone in their lakeside house when his death occurred. According to Elsie, Edgar was cleaning one of his pistols when it accidentally fired, and he died instantly of a gunshot to the head. Another popular theory, of course, was that the mentally compromised Elsie had shot and killed him. A third theory was that Edgar had become deeply depressed over his difficult life with Elsie and, after his war years, suffered from what we would now call post-traumatic stress disorder, so had taken his own life. While Elsie was never formally accused of killing Edgar, the cloud of suspicion that hung over her, her inability to take care of herself with Edgar gone, and her emotional instability inspired her to make her way to her mother's house, a day's travel away, and hang herself from a tree near the door.

When Bob Hope's most famous and final incarnation began in 1903, he brought with him from those lives his love of travel in pursuit of his interests, his delight in being a source of humor and entertainment, his devotion to the military and his wife, and his devout Catholicism. It's important to note that his wife in this life, Dolores, was most certainly *not* the reincarnation of his troubled partner Elsie, but his determination to provide beautifully for Dolores and his family was already deeply ingrained in him when he arrived from Home for the last time.

ROSEMARY CLOONEY

Beloved singer and actress Rosemary Clooney chose a difficult life for her fifty-fourth and final incarnation, proving to herself that she could succeed despite a number of personal challenges that had defeated her in the past.

A lifetime in the early 1800s was sadly typical. Her name was Margrit. She was born two months premature and narrowly escaped death from an umbilical cord wrapped around her throat. It was feared that there might be long-term effects from her brain having been deprived of oxygen, but except for being unusually small, she seemed to develop normally.

A second tragic disadvantage was the fact that she was born in a Swiss asylum. Her mother, Analiese, had murdered her father with a hatchet because he had accidentally dropped bread crumbs on a floor she'd just swept. She then had had her twelve-year-old son, Margrit's older brother, hide his father's body in a well while she burned down their house, so that no one would see the blood. The brother, distraught and terrified, had run to the home of his mother's older brother, an attorney, and told him what had happened. The uncle had been aware all his life of Analiese's mental fragility and finally found her kneeling beside a hidden forest stream, naked and singing quietly to herself as she tried to rinse the blood from her dress. He had had no trouble getting her declared legally insane rather than guilty of murder, and within days she'd been committed to an asylum, not knowing until weeks later that she was pregnant with Margrit.

Margrit and her brother were taken in by their uncle, his wife, and their three children, who were very kind to them. Margrit's brother, emotionally scarred from the events surrounding his father's death and genetically predisposed to mental illness, ran away two years later. In the meantime, after a great deal of medication and compassionate care, Analiese seemed to make a remarkable recovery in the asylum. On the condition that she live in a structured, supervised environment, Analiese was released into her brother's home and reunited with her then five-year-old daughter. To give her a sense of purpose as well as structure, her brother arranged for her to work in a music box factory owned by his friend, Thierry, where she seemed to thrive.

Life looked even more encouraging when Thierry and Analiese fell in love. He was fully aware of her past and convinced, as was her brother, that she had been successfully rehabilitated, so when the opportunity presented itself to open a second factory on the Swiss-Austrian border, the couple quickly married and moved to their new home two hundred miles away. They insisted on taking Margrit with them and, in the process, separated her from the only safety and security she'd ever known—an uncle, aunt, and cousins she'd lived with and loved all her life.

The little girl was understandably frightened, heartbroken, and deeply depressed to be uprooted by two people she barely knew, birth mother or not, and transplanted to a strange house in a strange town. Less out of concern for Margrit than in an effort to make Margrit easier to live with, Thierry and Analiese began giving her Analiese's medication, which emotionally muted her and created a chemical dependence that lasted throughout her brief lifetime.

They also saw to it that she continued the organ lessons she'd begun at her aunt and uncle's house. She had a great gift and a passionate love of music, particularly the compositions of Bach and Mozart. She could lose herself for hours on end, and when she allowed herself to dream at all, she hoped one day to become a concert organist and travel throughout Europe, where she might find a place she felt she belonged and, this time, couldn't be taken away against her will.

The dynamic in Margrit's home created an environment in which she perpetually felt like an outsider. Thierry insisted on control and structure at the factory and in his house, and Analiese adoringly complied. A vast majority of the time, it worked for them. On those rare occasions when Analiese showed signs of emotional imbalance, it was invariably because the structure of her life had been momentarily disrupted by Margrit's simple needs. All it took was more medication, and Margrit giving up and leaving her mother alone, to get Analiese back on track. But there seemed to be no place for Margrit to become part of the family rather than an extension of it. She developed a much deeper attachment to Thierry than to her mother; he didn't seem to love her, but he also didn't seem to dislike her either or become tense every time she walked into the room, as her mother did. She came to enjoy pleasing him and impressing him with her considerable talent at the organ, and she hoped that someday, if she behaved herself, tried hard enough, and, with the help of her mother's medication, caused little enough trouble, that she might win him over completely.

Unbeknownst to Margrit, her organ instructor, who was well connected throughout Europe, invited a few prestigious dignitaries to a recital at which sixteen-year-old Margrit performed. A few weeks later, a message arrived, offering her a scholarship to study music and musicology at the Sorbonne in Paris. She was ecstatic and breathlessly shared the news with Thierry. For the first time in her life, he gave her a hug—a rather stiff, awkward hug, but a hug nonetheless. Analiese walked in during the hug and flew into an instant, insane rage. She accused Margrit of having wanted Thierry for herself for years and of trying to replace her in his life. Now, she claimed, she had caught her in the act of trying to seduce him. She demanded that Margrit leave the house immediately and never return or she swore she would kill her. Margrit turned helplessly to Thierry to defend her and explain the perfectly innocent hug. Instead, forced to choose between a stepdaughter to whom he'd never been close and a wife who'd been his constant companion and of whom he had good reason to be afraid, he stood beside Analiese and said that yes, he thought it was time for Margrit to go. He then walked to open the door with his arm around his wife and simply said, "Get out."

Having nowhere else to go, Margrit fled to the home of her organ teacher, who'd always been kind, generous, and supportive. He and his wife took her in, arranged her passage to Paris and a place to stay until her classes at the Sorbonne began, and gave her enough money to get her safely there. Tragically, en route to Paris Margrit became desperately ill with what was actually withdrawal from years of addiction to her mother's medication. Her heart gave out just as her coach reached the outskirts of Paris.

Obviously her extraordinary musical talent came with her when she arrived for her incarnation as Rosemary Clooney. So did two of the key players in her lifetime as Margrit. One was Thierry. She was still trying to please him when she married him not once but twice, when he was known as José Ferrer. Neither marriage was a happy one. The other key player was her kind, generous, supportive organ teacher, known in her last incarnation as her close and loyal friend Bing Crosby. And the bipolar disorder and prescription drug addiction she battled throughout her life as Rosemary Clooney were classic examples of cell memory in action.

JOSEPH CAMPBELL

It's very rare that I run across anyone in this life, celebrity or "civilian," who was famous in a past life. When I learned from Francine that the brilliant mythologist, writer, and lecturer Joseph Campbell was the reincarnation of Plato, I was surprised, but only for a moment. The more I thought about it, the more it made perfect sense. Exquisite mind, a great passion for knowledge and learning, otherworldly wisdom—when you list the most memorable qualities of both men, it's impossible to tell which of them you're describing. How appropriate that they were both the same spirit.

Plato, of course, was one of this world's earliest philosophers, and the source of one of my favorite quotes: "We are nothing here but the shadows on the wall of the cave." He lived from approximately 427 to 347 BC, during the Age of Synthesis. With his two older brothers he became a student of Socrates, who taught them to critically challenge their beliefs as part of his basic premise that "the unexamined life is not worth living."

Plato was opposed to the Athenian democracy of the time and was tried and convicted of religious heresy and the corruption of youth. He was sentenced to death, but his friends freed him by paying a fine. The result of that experience was an understandable disenchantment with all existing political regimes and an insistence that politics could only be saved from uselessness if genuine philosophers attained political power, or if those in power became genuine philosophers.

In approximately 387 BC, Plato founded a university in Athens with a curriculum that included physical science, astronomy, mathematics, and philosophy. He presided over and lectured at the Academy, as it was called. During that time King Dionysius died. He was succeeded by his teenage son Dionysius II, whose uncle—a friend of Plato's—invited Plato to travel to Sicily to personally oversee the boy's studies. Plato accepted the invitation, seeing it as an opportunity to finally achieve the reality of a philosopher king. But, in the end, Dionysius II had no interest in becoming a philosopher, so Plato returned to his responsibilities at the Academy.

He was a prolific, sophisticated writer in his lives as both Plato and Joseph Campbell. Plato wrote thirty-six Socratic dialogues, which have been used to teach philosophy, ethics, rhetoric, logic, and mathematics. In his life as Joseph Campbell, he wrote more than fifty books that were influential in areas of mythology, art, philosophy, psychology, and literature. In both lifetimes, he was a highly respected and sought-after professor and lecturer. Though Plato's lectures were not recorded, Joseph Campbell's were, and they will continue to be studied and treasured for decades to come.

Joseph also spent a significant lifetime in the 1200s. It began in Sweden. His name was Henrik and, all things considered, it's no surprise that he'd charted himself to be born to two of that country's most renowned scholars. He'd spent his time on the Other Side between incarnations intensely researching everything about ancient Egypt, from the pharaohs to the politics to the pyramids, and almost from the time he could talk, Henrik was begging his parents to take him to Egypt. He would describe in uncanny detail the places he wanted to visit and study, sketching roadways and rivers and villages as if he'd seen them a thousand times before. Intrigued, his parents eventually arranged a trip to Egypt when Henrik was twelve. On that trip, they discovered that Henrik was able to interpret both cuneiforms and hieroglyphics on sight. Amazed at their son's abilities and open-minded enough to encourage him in every possible way, they relocated to Egypt and saw to it that Henrik was given an extraordinary education in archaeology, Egyptian theology, and his particular fascination, hieroglyphics. He became a great scholar, teacher, and researcher, living a simple life on the outskirts of Cairo and leading countless expeditions to the Great Pyramids of Giza, sharing the vast wealth of his knowledge and his endless curiosity with the students who traveled from the far corners of Africa, Europe, and Asia to study with him.

One of those students was a very bright, pretty, young Danish woman named Madja. Henrik had never intended to marry, believing it would be unfair to ask any woman to compete with his love of learning and teaching. But Madja shared his passions and understood him perfectly. The two of them were married when Henrik was forty-one and Madja was nineteen.

Their lives together couldn't have been busier, happier, and more stimulating. It was a devastating loss to Madja and the whole Egyptian scholastic community when Henrik passed away at the age of forty-seven from typhoid fever. Madja proudly continued their work until her death in her early nineties.

The two of them were reunited in this world when they were known as Joseph Campbell and his wife, Jean Erdman, who met and recognized each other instantly when she had been one of his comparative literature students at Sarah Lawrence College. Their marriage lasted for forty-nine years, until his death in 1987.

He lived a breathtaking fifty-nine lifetimes on earth, and he'll continue expanding his vast knowledge at Home from now on, as determined as he's been since his life as Plato to infuse the great minds of this world with the concept that only true philosophers belong in political office.

JACK LALANNE

One of history's most influential fitness and nutrition experts, Jack LaLanne left this world a much better place than how he found it when his third and final incarnation ended on January 23, 2011. And his is a fascinating story of cell memory in action.

His first lifetime on earth began in the mid-1700s in what is now Florida. His name was Severino (his nickname, Seve), and he was a forceps baby—forceps were used to help pull his head from the birth canal, causing what was then called "cerebral paralysis" but has come to be known as cerebral palsy. His mother, Elena, didn't survive giving birth to him. His grief-stricken father, Paolo, irrationally blamed Seve for Elena's death, and gave the baby to his aunt to raise while he returned to his native Spain, never to see his son again.

Seve's aunt, Luz, was a godsend. She had no idea how to treat cerebral paralysis, nor did anyone else back then, but she knew how to be loving and kind and how to give her new child the self-confidence that comes from being unconditionally adored. Luz had never married, and she earned a modest living as a seamstress, feeding herself and Seve primarily vegetables from her small garden, fruit from the trees near her tiny house, and fish from a nearby stream. By necessity rather than by design, Seve's diet kept him as healthy as possible, and as he grew into a smart, well-mannered, determined boy, he took it upon himself—with his aunt's encouragement—to try strengthening and rehabilitating his body. While he never achieved any form of self-sufficiency, he never gave up, never felt sorry for himself, and until he died at the age of twenty-one, never stopped believing that someday he would be able to walk.

The second of his three lives began in the mid-1840s. His name was Chester, and he was one of four sons born in eastern Pennsylvania to a couple who owned and traveled with a relatively new form of entertainment called a carnival. Almost from the time they were old enough to walk and talk, Chester and his brothers were trained to be carnival barkers, enthusiastically drawing crowds to the available games, shows, contests, and displays on the midway. They sang, they danced, they juggled, they shouted, and they waved. The small, confident Chester, in particular, had a smile and a charisma that made whatever he was pitching sound irresistible. Travel and the family business kept the boys from being formally educated, but their mother taught them to read and write, and they were generally well cared for, happy children.

When Chester was sixteen he married a girl named Molly, the daughter of his parents' partner in the carnival business. Shortly after the wedding, he and his older brother enlisted in the Union army. They were side by side on the battlefield when his brother was killed and Chester was shot in the back, leaving him paralyzed

from the chest down. Chester fought hard to overcome his paralysis and developed considerable upper-
body strength with a series of weights and pulleys his
father devised for him in their home on the outskirts of
Harrisburg. Molly was completely devoted to her husband despite his paralysis, and being a devout Christian,
she introduced him to the Bible and his innate spiritual
nature. She'd sit at his bedside every night and read him
his favorite psalms and Bible stories until he fell asleep.

That incarnation ended by blood poisoning when
Chester was thirty-eight. Thanks to Molly's loving
efforts, he left this world utterly confident that he was
going Home and grateful for the life he'd had. At his
funeral service, Molly read aloud to the congregation
Isaiah 40:31, the Bible verse that had most inspired him
and lifted him up when discouragement threatened to
penetrate too deeply:

> But they that wait upon the Lord
> shall renew their strength;
> they shall mount up with wings as eagles;
> they shall run, and not be weary;
> and they shall walk, and not faint.

When he returned to earth in 1916 in the persona
of Jack LaLanne, he became a virtual poster child for

the power of cell memory. He was born into a healthy body, but his two past lives had essentially taught him that being incarnated means being debilitated for one reason or another and then struggling to overcome that debilitation. When nature didn't debilitate him, he saw to it in his early life that he debilitated himself. He overloaded his body with unhealthy food and took no care of himself at all, with the result that he was, by his own admission, short-tempered, bulimic, and the victim of chronic headaches. He was fifteen when a Paul Bragg lecture on health and nutrition inspired him to "let the healing begin." His spirit mind had never forgotten the beautiful Bible verse that had ignited his soul in his previous life, and from his mid-teens on he lived by it.

His deep belief in God's message of "doing unto others" and his gift of persuasion carried over from his carnival days in the 1800s, propelling him to share his passion for physical fitness with the world, both by motivation and by example. Finally he'd been blessed with a body that was unencumbered by injury and illness. He celebrated that fact and repaid that blessing every day by honoring his body in every way and inspiring millions of people around the world, many who are still thriving today because of his influence.

And by his side for the last fifty-one of his ninety-six years, and during his third and final incarnation, was his wife, Elaine, to whom he'd been happily married once before, when her name was Molly. Those who knew them often commented that they seemed as if they were meant to be together. And of course they were—they had charted it themselves on the Other Side, long before they came here this time around.

INGRID BERGMAN

On August 29, 1982, the exquisite and controversial actress Ingrid Bergman went Home to the Other Side for the forty-sixth and final time. Her last incarnation was filled with great acclaim and equally great scandal. It took every one of her previous lifetimes to build the strength it took to survive such highs and lows, let alone with such resolute dignity.

It was the late fifteenth century when Ingrid's lifetime in Kyoto, Japan, began. Her name was Sachi, and she was the only child of a strict, traditional Shinto couple. She was delicate, shy, almost pathologically obedient, and eager to please.

She'd also been raised to be an exemplary wife and mother. Sachi was thirty-one when her parents deemed it appropriate for her to marry and found the proper husband for her. He was a friend of Sachi's father and a highly decorated, retired military officer whose position dictated the presence of a dutiful wife and an heir.

Ten months after the wedding, Sachi proudly presented her new husband with a son. Jun was the light of his father's life. He was also Sachi's first experience with deep, all-encompassing love. Neither she nor her husband had ever pretended to feel or expect love between them, although they treated each other with perfect respect. Sachi's adoration for her baby boy, though, took her breath away. She'd never known that she was even capable of loving someone to the depth of her soul. So she didn't mind a bit that her husband wanted nothing to do with such basics as feeding, bathing, diapering, and holding Jun and left those joys to her. Her husband swelled with pride when he showed off Jun to his friends and relatives, and once or twice Sachi saw tears of joy in his eyes when he watched Jun sleep. She never thought more highly of him than during his moments of unguarded tenderness with a son, who resembled his father more with each passing day.

Jun was four years old when he very suddenly died of pneumonia. Sachi's husband was traveling at the time, and the shock of returning home to find that his precious boy had passed away was devastating. Compounding the tragedy was that he not only failed to acknowledge Sachi's equally consuming grief, he also blamed her terribly unfairly for Jun's death. He began arranging long "business" trips far away from her so that he could tell himself he hadn't been dishonorable enough to actually leave her.

Alone and disconsolate, Sachi reached out to her parents but was stunned when they turned her away. They were ashamed of her for not taking good enough care of her only child and for not being able to keep her husband content enough to stay home.

Her despair finally overwhelmed her. With nothing else to live for and no resources of her own with which to regroup and move on, she deliberately starved herself to death, dying two years to the day after the death of her son.

Ingrid returned very quickly to a life in Egypt. Her name was Bast, and at the age of fourteen, thanks to her father's political connections, she became a trusted companion and lady-in-waiting to the queen. Either luckily or unluckily for Bast, the queen had a brother who was both impossibly handsome and very powerful behind the scenes. He was already committed to a loveless but politically advantageous betrothal, but that didn't stop him from secretly pursuing Bast. She was young, flattered, and thrilled by the drama and danger of this forbidden love. They began an intensely passionate affair, carried out in whatever hidden places they could find.

Within two months his betrothed, who'd become suspicious and was having him followed, uncovered the affair. Bast was immediately taken away to a small, isolated cell until a hearing was held before a tribunal of four heavily robed men, none of whom ever revealed their names or titles. She was proclaimed guilty of treason (i.e., threatening a marriage the tribunal considered imperative to the future of Egypt). Rather than execute her, which they were afraid might attract too much attention, the men of the tribunal sent her away to work in the wheat fields on the banks of the Nile River "until the threat had passed." A guard would be watching her constantly, she was told, in case she tried to escape, although she would never be aware of his presence or his identity.

Her exile lasted for almost two lonely, backbreaking years, when one of the robed men appeared with no warning and informed her that she was being allowed to return to the queen's service. She was escorted back to the palace, where everything had changed. Her former lover, the queen's brother, had married and moved away with his bride to a distant, undisclosed location. He'd never been told or had even asked where Bast had gone, and she never saw or heard from him again. The queen, who'd once been kind to her and had trusted her, was now cold and abusive toward her. She had requested Bast's return in order to exact slow revenge for what she considered to be Bast's calculated betrayal of her position as queen.

Bast remained essentially a captive servant to the queen and an outcast throughout the palace for her five remaining decades there. For solace, she became a devout Muslim and spent many hours a day in private prayer, in search of the forgiveness she couldn't seem to find on earth. When death came, just a month before the death of the queen, it was never clearly established whether she had accidentally fallen from a balcony of the palace onto the stone courtyard below or had jumped. Whichever it had been, she was relieved to return Home after yet another lifetime in which she'd faced worldly shame and been defeated by it.

The same could not be said of Ingrid Bergman, who, in the end, refused to be defeated again when scandal hit. I have to admit I was surprised not to find Roberto Rossellini, the lover with whom she'd created that scandal, in any of her past lives. Instead, I found Jun, who was back again with Ingrid in the persona of her and Roberto's daughter, Isabella, so that they could have more time on earth together and Isabella could be of help to her this time around, when the public temporarily turned away from her.

It's worth adding that Ingrid's work on the Other Side involves her being an Orientator who specializes in young women arriving Home as a result of suicide.

JAMES CAGNEY

Considered by many to be one of the greatest actors in film history, James Cagney was a very private, hardworking, multifaceted man whose thirty-fifth and final incarnation ended in 1986. His childhood in poverty, his work ethic, his widely varied interests—ranging from performing to farming to sailing—along with his passion for losing himself in the characters he portrayed as an actor all came naturally to him from the past lives he charted as his soul's earthly journey progressed.

Around 1830, he and his fraternal twin sister were born to a farming couple in eastern Indiana. Named Charles and Beth, they were very close and thought living on a farm was the most idyllic life anyone could hope for. Unfortunately, their father didn't seem to appreciate the treasure of living on a few acres of inherited farmland as much as his children did. He was an incurably lazy, irresponsible man who, on the rare occasions when he had two dimes to rub together, would spend all his money at the tavern in the nearby town. The farm was in a constant state of overgrown disrepair, and when they were as young as four years old, Charles and Beth took it upon themselves to pull weeds in the fields and tend to the vegetables, which were often the family's only source of food.

Their mother was a weak woman who had resigned herself to a lonely, meager life with a husband she'd married only to escape her parents' strictness. She now found herself trapped and struggling to raise two unplanned children essentially on her own—"your children," as their father typically called them, as if they were entirely their mother's idea and their mother's fault. Charles and Beth did their best to help her around the house and keep up their mother's spirits. Her perpetual feeling of helplessness prompted her to almost obsessively read the Bible, but rather than taking some initiative to change her and her children's lives for the better, she would assure them, "God will take care of us. Just you wait and see."

Charles gravitated instead toward the maxim, "God helps those who help themselves," whether or not he'd ever actually heard it. When he was ten years old, he went to the local barbershop, where his father was getting a haircut. When he thought no one was looking, he reached into the cigar box where the owner kept the shop's proceeds and stole a handful of coins. He wanted to buy his mother a birthday gift. But he was caught before he reached the door. His father, claiming embarrassment but, in truth, simply not wanting to take a chance on being held responsible, promptly left. The barber, who sympathized with Charles and Beth's situation, said he would let the matter drop right then and there if Charles promised to work off the amount of the attempted theft. Charles kept that promise and proved to be such a conscientious worker that the barber hired him to clean up and do odd jobs, then eventually taught him barber skills.

Charles quickly discovered how unlike his father he really was. He loved the satisfaction of working, and he loved earning money. He began going from one business in town to another, applying for any work they might have to offer, as long as it didn't conflict with his hours at the barbershop. He was hired at the saloon to clean up and do odd jobs as well, and soon—at first for his own amusement and then for the amusement of the patrons—he found he was able to perfectly mimic the showgirls' dance steps and memorize their routines. He would occasionally perform in drag onstage, chorus-line style with the other dancers, to the audience's great hilarity. It earned him generous tips. One of the luxuries of his life, he would always recall, was that he could be completely lost in the moment while he was performing. There was no lazy, irresponsible, neglectful father in his life, no weak, fearful mother, no parched "weed farm" far beyond help. There was just music, fun, and laughter, and he cherished those brief escapes.

By the time he was eighteen Charles had earned and saved a considerable amount of money. His sister, Beth, had also been diligently taking in embroidery and needlepoint work during the past three years. The two of them used some of their earnings to take care of their mother, but they refused to give a red cent to their father, knowing it would disappear at the local tavern in the blink of an eye.

One day a once-in-a-lifetime opportunity landed in Charles's lap. A regular customer at the barbershop, who'd befriended Charles and greatly admired his barbering skills and his work ethic, announced that he was heading west to make his fortune in the California gold rush. His offer: if Charles would come with him, they would become equal partners in a barbershop that was bound to be wildly successful in this brand new, exciting territory, where there were probable fortunes to be made.

Charles agreed, on the condition that he could bring his sister and mother with him. Beth immediately accepted the invitation. She was definitely ready to spread her wings. Plus, she knew her talents with a needle and thread would be appreciated out west. But their mother declined, using the excuse "your father needs me" and ultimately just too resigned to muster the energy. Her children left her with the key to a hidden lockbox of money, which would have lasted her for years if she hadn't given it to her husband to keep him happy. He drank and gambled it away on the tavern's new roulette wheel.

The gold rush was everything Charles and Beth had dreamed of and much, much more. Charles's barbershop was bustling every minute of every day, and Beth had all the seamstress jobs she could handle. They ended up settling in a small town on the northern California coast, where Charles bought a second barbershop, a saloon where he entertained two nights a week, and a small well-tended farm on which he loved to work and for which he hired a team of reliable day laborers who appreciated having the jobs. He also bought a small sailboat, now that he'd been exposed to and fallen in love with the ocean.

Beth met and married a successful prospector, who'd come for the gold rush from his home in Delaware, and together they built a house within walking distance of Charles's farm. Charles, on the other hand, considered himself married to his freedom, his wide variety of jobs, and his many hobbies. He was actively opposed to becoming a father. "How would I know the first thing about being a good father," he would ask Beth, "when the only one I've ever known was such a failure?"

Despite the onset of several illnesses—including arthritis, dangerously high blood pressure, and chronic asthma—Charles kept right on sailing, farming, entertaining at his saloon (from a chair onstage), and occasionally cutting hair at his barbershop until he passed away at the age of fifty-eight. He came roaring back after just a few short years, in 1899, as James Cagney, bringing with him the woman he admired most from all his previous incarnations, his sister Beth. Her name was now Billie Vernon. They married in 1922, and they were still married sixty-four years later, when he went Home for the last time, after leaving an indelible mark on this earth.

JOHN RITTER

It won't surprise anyone who knew him that John Ritter is a very advanced soul. His fifty-first and final incarnation ended on September 11, 2003, and he left this earth suddenly but so at peace with the life he had lived and so looking forward to returning to his life at Home. Never forget that from the point of view of the spirits on the Other Side, who are able to perceive our souls' journeys in the context of eternity, we'll all be together again in the blink of an eye. So they understand far better than we on earth do the difference between missing someone and being excited about seeing someone again very soon.

One of John's earliest lives took place immediately after the time of Christ. His name was Seth, and he became a close friend of the apostle Matthew, who shared the word of Jesus with him and transformed him from lost and hollow to spiritually enlightened. He found his path and devoted himself to the needs of the poor, the sick, and the godless. Eventually, he made his way to Amalfi, where he joined a group of Essenes, an early Christian sect that renounced materialism and other worldly pursuits and focused exclusively on religious disciplines. While some Essenes practiced celibacy, Seth was part of a commune that allowed marriage, conditional on a three-year courtship. After the appropriate waiting period, Seth married an Essenian woman named Rebecca, with whom he had three children. He became a devout, gifted ministerial leader, unique in his refreshing readiness to share the joy of God's word with smiles and humor rather than somber heaviness. His kindness and charitable works attracted dozens of followers and became a true inspiration to his children. His daughter, Sarah, became a renowned healer in Ein Gedi, an oasis on the shore of the Dead Sea.

Seth's faith was challenged again and again as, one by one, he lost his wife and two of his children. Desolate as he was, he never wavered in his certainty that they were whole, happy, and blissful in Christ's arms on the Other Side, and he and his daughter Sarah became even more committed to their ministries with each heartbreaking loss. Seth evolved into a great God-centered grief counselor in his later years and passed away quietly of heart disease at the miraculous age of eighty-two. Another of John's many exemplary incarnations began in the early 1800s. His name was Martin, and his father had moved the family to the relative wilderness of what is now known as Montana in search of open spaces and new challenges. Martin's father was a lawyer, and Martin, who deeply loved and admired him, followed in his footsteps so that the two of them could set up a modest practice together. Family money made it possible for them to take on pro bono cases when the need arose, as it often did, or when they believed their clients' rights were being violated, whether those clients could pay in full or not.

I should mention that when each of us writes our chart for an upcoming incarnation, we choose a life theme, which is the specific purpose that defines our intended goal. There are forty-four life themes. John's chosen theme for his lifetime as Martin was justice. Justice was his driving force and his passion, as it was his father's. They would have had a much more comfortable, predictable life back home in Virginia, but the power of their shared life theme demanded that they go where their souls told them they were needed.

When they first arrived in their new home, they worked tirelessly to spread the word that they'd set up a practice, and they worked even harder when clients began showing up. Martin would travel long hours on horseback to meet with clients who couldn't make it to the law office they'd established behind their farmhouse.

During those travels Martin met his wife, Helen, whose father he represented in a land dispute. Martin and Helen built a house on Martin's family's property and they had two children. They felt blessed. At Martin's insistence, they never sat down to a meal without offering a prayer of thanks. Nor did they ever miss a Sunday service at the modest chapel a few miles from their home. When Martin's father became ill and was forced to retire, Martin took over the law practice, and the family united in lovingly caring for Martin's parents until the two of them had passed away.

Martin, Helen, and their children became involved with the white settlement of St. Mary's Mission and, through the mission and their own efforts, gained the trust of the Iroquois and other Native American tribes. Martin helped bridge the cultural gaps between them by organizing and performing in pageants celebrating Christian holidays and events in the life of Christ—Christmas, Easter, the Sermon on the Mount, the raising of Lazarus from the dead, and others. Martin was deeply moved by the experience of uniting an audience full of disparate people through the simple power of shared emotion and, to our good fortune, the impact of that experience stayed with him into his lifetime as John Ritter.

Martin didn't care that he created some enemies for himself by helping the Iroquois regain some of the lands that had been poached from them by unscrupulous settlers, who felt entitled to that land simply because they said so. He saved the farm of a struggling, hardworking widower with six children, whose brother was trying to cheat him out of it with some forged documents. He made peace between two spinster sisters who'd hated each other for years over what turned out to be a misinterpreted clause in their father's will. With every case

Martin took on, no matter how high or low the stakes, he literally invested his heart.

The inevitable, relentless stress slowly began weakening his heart, though, which had been compromised already during previous incarnations. Martin insisted on dismissing any symptoms as exhaustion, and said he would take better care as soon as a current case was resolved. His justice theme wouldn't allow him to maintain objectivity about whatever client or cause had incited his passion, so it was possibly appropriate—even predictable—that the heart attack that killed him at the age of fifty-eight, and weakened his heart again in his final incarnation, happened while he sat at his desk in the middle of the night, hard at work on a mediation in which children were being pulled between their warring parents.

John brought his father from that incarnation with him for his last years on earth. This time, he was his beloved older brother, Tom—a lawyer in his most recent lifetime too—who, by the way, had himself tested after John died and discovered that he had the same congenital aortic tear that had killed his brother. Tom's surgery for that tear was successful, and he's doing well. It's not an overstatement to say that John's death saved his brother's life, and considering the past life they shared together in the Montana region and the chart John wrote for himself in this one, he wouldn't have had it any other way.

KAREN CARPENTER

The forty-ninth incarnation of the gifted singer and drummer Karen Carpenter ended in 1983, when she was only thirty-two, and she'll be back twice more. I've always wished that I could have done a past-life regression with her, to help her unearth the points of entry that allowed anorexia to overtake her life and ultimately kill her. It's often but not always true that disorders like anorexia are deeply ingrained precisely because they're rooted in one or more past lives, and unless the core of the problem is exposed so that the mind can process it, it's almost impossible to heal.

The first lifetime in which weight was an issue for Karen—through no fault of her own—took place in seventeenth-century India. Her name was Rani. Because of an injury during her birth, she was paralyzed from the waist down. According to her parents' beliefs, it was a sign that Rani was cursed. While her parents wanted her taken care of, they also wanted her as far away from them and their other children as possible. They were financially advantaged enough to be able to place her in an institution, to which they paid significant fees for her food and care, but they never even considered visiting her. In fact, the last time Rani saw her parents in her brief life was when she was four weeks old.

Rani was confined to her bed and a wooden wheelchair from the time she would have been old enough to walk. She was given no physical therapy and no schooling, although one of the nurses did teach her to read. The priorities at the institution were to keep their patients as content and compliant as possible, which in Rani's case translated to supplying her with plenty of food and books, the only two things in an otherwise monotonous life that she looked forward to. The greatest happiness she knew was sitting in her wheelchair under a tree on the institution's grounds, reading one of her beloved history books and enjoying a generous meal.

Living as she was on a seemingly endless supply of carbohydrate-rich foods, without a moment of exercise, it was inevitable that Rani was morbidly obese by the age of twelve. The staff could no longer lift Rani from her chair to her bed. They tried from time to time, with a lot of groaning, insults, and name-calling that hurt Rani deeply, but eventually the staff limited Rani's life to the hard wooden wheelchair that she'd long since outgrown. She was virtually unable to sleep for more than an hour or two at a time, due to the relent-less discomfort of the chair, and she developed pain-ful sores. It's no surprise that she was grateful when, before her thirteenth birthday, she passed away from obesity-related heart disease. She returned Home with cell memories of a weakened heart and the lesson that being overweight means pain, ridicule, loneliness, and an early death.

She was born healthy, tall, beautiful, and slender in France in the mid-1800s. Her name was Gabrielle, and this time around her parents adored her. The family lived in a traditional home. Her father was a success-ful jeweler, and she and her mother were respectfully submissive. Gabrielle's father was a bright, responsible, kind man with a wonderful sense of humor, and her mother was a charming woman with a musical laugh who was still as in love with her husband as she'd been the day she'd married him. They saw to it that their daughter had a first-class education, and on the completion of finishing school when she was eighteen, Gabrielle met François, a twenty-two-year-old law stu-dent and the brother of one of her classmates. It was love at first sight for both of them, and they were mar-ried six months later, with the enthusiastic approval of both of their families. Knowing their daughter was in good hands, Gabrielle's parents left to fulfill their longtime dream of traveling the world at their leisure, and Gabrielle and François set up housekeeping in a charming apartment his parents had purchased for them as a wedding gift.

Several months into their marriage, François made a confession to Gabrielle: he was only studying law to satisfy his parents' wish that he graduate and join his father's law firm. But he was only going through the motions. He had a dream of his own, which he wanted to pursue with Gabrielle's help and support. He believed that he had the talent and passion to be a great fashion designer. With Gabrielle as his model, he was sure they could both be very successful. Gabrielle, wanting to be supportive, didn't tell him that she had no interest in being a model, although she did remind him that she knew nothing about modeling. No problem, he assured her. Swept up in her husband's excitement at first, Gabrielle agreed and began training and following François's strict regimen toward his definition of perfection.

When he wasn't dictating every minute detail of Gabrielle's transformation, François was busy designing an array of gowns he was sure would secure his status in the world of haute couture. Finally satisfied that his premiere collection was ready and that his model wife was well trained and bone-thin enough to show his collection off to its best advantage, he bought his way into a minor fashion show at a Paris hotel.

The reviews were tepid at best, and François was furious. The problem couldn't possibly be his designs, he was sure. That left only one place to lay the blame. It had to be Gabrielle who had failed to impress the critics, and he wasn't about to let it happen again. He hired a new trainer for her, and a new hair stylist and makeup artist, but most of all he became obsessively brutal about her diet and exercise regimen, taking her measurements and weighing her every morning and punishing her by withholding food entirely and cruelly insulting her if she'd gained so much as an ounce. With her parents away and François now methodically isolating her from her friends, Gabrielle had no one around to point out that, contrary to her husband's claims, his success was not dependent on how little she weighed; it was very probable that he was simply untalented and should head back to law school where he belonged.

François and Gabrielle traveled throughout Europe as he bought his way into one fashion show after another, but his designs were met with resounding apathy from the critics. In Florence Gabrielle stepped off the stage and collapsed of heart failure. Already programmed from a past incarnation to equate excess weight with pain and loneliness, she died in Italy at the age of twenty-nine, five feet ten inches tall and eighty-seven pounds, with the message that even an extra ounce on her body could destroy her potential success and the success of someone she loved.

It was very much to Karen Carpenter's credit that after becoming a highly respected performer and celebrity, she spoke out about her anorexia, which encouraged other celebrities to open up about their own eating disorders. Doing so saved a lot of lives. It's precisely because her soul finally released that pain that she'll return for her next life healed from her illness and ready to become the superstar she's already planning to be, but this time a superstar in the medical profession.

It's also important to emphasize that no one significant from her past lives reappeared in the lifetime of Karen Carpenter.

PETER SELLERS

The brilliantly gifted, complicated spirit we knew as Peter Sellers left this world for the fortieth time in 1980 and will be back three more times. Like so many people who are deeply spiritual but have difficulty with relationships here on earth, his conflicts were rooted in previous incarnations, and he'll continue reincarnating until those conflicts are resolved.

One of his more significant past lives took place in France in the early 1600s. He was the sixth of eight children born to a devoutly religious Catholic couple, and he eagerly entered the priesthood with the best of intentions and the added bonus of his own deep spirituality, which included a gift for seeing and communicating with the spirit world. He'd discovered early in his life that neither his parents nor the nuns and priests who had taught him as he was growing up were receptive to hearing about his gift, which he'd found enormously confusing. So he'd dutifully kept his special abilities to himself without ever quite understanding why they were perceived as sacrilege rather than an affirmation of the life-after-death truth that he'd been taught to believe in as a good Catholic.

Father Claude, as he was called, was a popular priest, devout and compassionate, and especially gifted with children, who were drawn to his patience, his playfulness, and his unique insistence on the importance of laughter as part of a well-rounded life. It was because of his friendship with the children of the church that his life and his future lives were wounded.

The parents of a nine-year-old boy summoned Father Claude to their house one day. Their son—a normally happy, outgoing child—had been frightened and crying since he'd come home from school, and had refused to talk or come out of his room. They knew he loved and trusted Father Claude, and they hoped their son might confide in him, since they were getting nowhere in finding out what had so clearly traumatized him.

After a few hours with the boy, Father Claude learned, to his horror, that the child had been molested by the very powerful, politically connected monsignor of the church. Father Claude's heart was broken by this unspeakable cruelty, and he promised to take immediate action to see to it that the boy would be protected and the monsignor would be properly punished.

He reported this obscenity to his superiors, following every protocol along the way. His reward for doing the right thing was that the monsignor's powerful position in the Catholic hierarchy never diminished in the slightest while Father Claude was excommunicated from the church. He spent the next six years of his life unsuccessfully trying to find justice for that innocent child, even traveling to the Vatican and pleading for an audience with the pope, but he was rebuffed and ignored at every turn.

Compounding the tragedy, when the boy was fifteen years old, he managed to sneak into the monsignor's living quarters one night and kill him while he slept.

He made no effort to run away and was still standing beside the man's bed holding the knife when the other priests, who'd heard the monsignor's first screams of pain and fear, came rushing into the room.

The monsignor was given the holiest of funeral masses and buried in a place of most hallowed Catholic honor. The boy was executed. And Father Claude spent the rest of his life in bitter seclusion in Switzerland, unable to reconcile the vast chasm between his spiritual convictions and the profane ways in which they were twisted by mankind.

Father Claude never lost his ability to see and converse with the spirit world, but that remained a source of confusion rather than a source of comfort for him. All he'd learned about it from those who were supposed to have instructed, inspired, and elevated him to his greatest spiritual potential was that his communication with spirits was, at best, inappropriate, and the less said about it the better. He died at the age of seventy, still deeply and privately clinging to his beliefs and his spirit-centered gifts but irreparably cynical about his fellow man. He also never forgave himself for breaking the promise he'd made to that nine-year-old boy. He wasn't even slightly consoled by the knowledge that he'd fought fiercely to do the right thing or that he'd lost due to powers and circumstances that were far beyond his control. The disparity between his spiri-tuality and his unease with humankind followed him from one lifetime to another to another, and it's one of the issues he'll be back to resolve.

He was able to be much more open and feel more accepted for his paranormal experiences during his life in Illinois as a man named Clark in the 1800s. Both his mother and his grandmother were spiritualists and they nurtured his gifts. He was proud to be the only one of the three of them who received regular visits and mes-sages from his father, who had died when Clark was two years old. In this lifetime, Clark was an introvert but fascinated by human behavior, studying the quirks and mannerisms of even the most ordinary people around him and teaching himself to mimic them perfectly, to the great delight of his mother and grandmother.

His other great fascination also became his life's work: from the moment he first saw a train, he was obsessed with everything to do with the newly arriving railroad system. He had a natural talent for mechanics and enjoyed a long, happy career building and repair-ing steam engines. His introverted nature and his innate hesitation to deeply connect with people led to two failed marriages, both of them childless, and he died alone of a heart attack in that lifetime at the age of fifty-two.

His incarnation as Peter Sellers reflected his ongoing passion for the paranormal, his difficulty with relationships, and most certainly his gift for creating the characters he portrayed as an actor by immersing himself in even the tiniest details of their behavior. It's also possible that there was a connection between Peter Sellers's love of cars and his past-life love of steam engines. The cell memory of a weakened heart ended his most recent lifetime in 1980 when he was only fifty-four. I'm sure those who knew him well would confirm that he'd actually begun bracing for his death as he approached the age of fifty-two, and that in the end he was looking forward to going Home.

LORETTA YOUNG

Loretta Young's fortieth lifetime on earth ended in the year 2000, and she'll be back for four more incarnations before she considers the worldly part of her soul's journey complete. Her sincere Catholic faith, her charismatic personality, and her compassion for the less fortunate have been at odds for centuries with her burdens of temptation, secrecy, and her occasional crises of faith, all of which she'll begin to address when she returns in 2016.

In the early 1300s, Loretta—then called Elsa—was the fifth child of a devoutly Catholic clockmaker and his wife, a baker, in southern Germany. She was their only daughter and very beautiful. Her parents' greatest hope was that Elsa become a teaching nun in the Benedictine order so that her beauty would not lead her to a vain, self-absorbed life of sin. To their profound relief, she was happy to commit herself to her church and her education. She also, from an early age, demonstrated a deep concern for the well-being of others. She would routinely leave half of her meals untouched, asking her mother to give the rest to "hungry children who haven't been as blessed as I have."

When she was ten years old, Elsa entered a convent some distance from home, where she was impeccably educated. She flawlessly adhered to the daily rituals of worship and was a particular favorite of one of the nuns, who took regular charitable trips to a nearby village to deliver donated food and clothing to the needy. Elsa loved accompanying the nun on these visits, gratified by the opportunity to perform tangible acts of kindness, which supplemented the many prayers the convent routinely devoted to the physically, emotionally, and spiritually bereft. When she was in her mid-teens, Elsa expanded her participation in charitable work, thanks to specific training at the convent. She taught families rudimentary vegetable gardening, goat milking, and rainwater conservation, as well as hymns and prayers. She attracted several novitiates for the convent during her local travels and became one of the area's most highly respected, highly valued nuns.

A skilled wood carver named Karl had been commissioned by the convent to replace their worn, unstable banisters with sturdy mahogany ones, with a cross carved into each newel. Karl was a quiet, very private man, but friendly and with a ready smile. He kept to himself as he worked long hours, day after day, week after week. He and Elsa saw each other regularly at the convent and, while they had never become more than passing acquaintances, they shared a great mutual regard. She admired his extraordinary work ethic and his pride in his wife and child, who he always spoke of with such love, and he, because he lived in the village, admired her for the countless acts of compassion she'd performed for his friends and neighbors.

One day, for the first time, Karl failed to show up for work. Word quickly reached the concerned residents of the convent that Karl's house had burned down during the night, and his wife and child had died in the fire. The entire convent, including Elsa, reached out to him, gave him shelter, food, and spiritual comfort to help him through the devastating tragedy, and a few weeks later he was able to move back into the work shed behind his house, which had escaped the flames, and finish his job at the convent.

Once he had left, Elsa began checking in on him on her regular trips into the village. For the most part, he seemed to be slowly recovering, finding comfort in building a new, much more modest home for himself on his property and most certainly in Elsa's visits. She brought food. She delivered the Eucharist, or Holy Communion. She prayed with him. She listened. She reassured. Over the next several months the two of them became incredibly close, and she began looking forward to those visits every bit as much as he did. Neither of them ever acknowledged to themselves that there was also a growing physical attraction between them. Elsa's unenhanced beauty was made even more breathtaking by her complete lack of awareness of it, and Karl's rough-hewn handsomeness was due in part to the extraordinary sensitivity in his hazel eyes. An attraction was unthinkable, but that didn't mean it didn't exist.

The night that changed everything, from which Elsa would still be recovering many lifetimes later, started when she arrived as usual at Karl's home with a small basket of bread and homegrown vegetables. She became alarmed when, despite the fact that she could vaguely hear noises inside, Karl didn't answer her knock at the door. She then tentatively opened the door and found him slumped against the wall of his small living space, quietly sobbing. She hurried to kneel beside him and comfort him. His grief, he explained a bit apologetically, hit him in waves, periodically overwhelming him, and the last thing he intended was for her to see him like this, after all her help and prayers and after what should have been more than enough time to heal. Elsa held him and promised to stay with him until this particular wave of pain had passed.

To their mutual shock and shame, by the time she left at sunrise the next morning, they had willingly consummated their friendship and, in both of their minds, committed a mortal sin. In a brief, painful conversation before she left, Karl volunteered to move far away as soon as possible to insure they would never have to face each other again, and she agreed that it would be for the best. He was gone two days later.

Elsa's horror at what she'd done consumed her. Her reputation at the convent was so impeccably elevated that she couldn't even bring herself to address this unspeakable sin at confession. Nor did she feel worthy enough to kneel before the altar and beg God for forgiveness. She went about her charitable work in the village as best she could for several days but was simply going through the motions. Everyone at the convent, with the best intentions, began asking her what was wrong, why the light in her eyes had vanished, and why she had become so sad and withdrawn.

It was a month later when her pain and loneliness became unbearable and, at the age of twenty-seven, she hanged herself in her tiny room overlooking the statue of Saint Benedict in the courtyard of the convent. She never knew that in taking her own life, she also took the life of the fetus growing inside her womb. Karl died of tuberculosis fifteen years later in northern Poland, unaware of Elsa's suicide.

Elsa wandered the convent and the village as an earthbound for almost two centuries. As with all ghosts, she had made a conscious decision to turn away from the tunnel that would take her Home. She was convinced that because she'd broken her vow of celibacy and then committed the mortal sin of suicide, God would most certainly turn her away and condemn her to an eternity in hell. (Please believe me, God never turns away from *anyone*, and there is no such thing as hell.) Finally, as happens with all earthbounds who are not "talked to the Light" by compassionate souls on earth, she was retrieved by spirits on the Other Side who knew of her pain and welcomed her into their—and God's—open, loving, forgiving arms.

Of course, one of the defining tragedies in the private life of the still devoutly Catholic Loretta Young was the child she conceived with the married Clark Gable and the many secrets that surrounded the birth and life of that child. Her insistence on not giving in to her fear and shame by taking her own life this time around but on living with them and through them instead shows a courage she didn't have before. She trusted God's love enough to step immediately and joyfully into the tunnel when ovarian cancer ended her life.

MONTGOMERY CLIFT

Montgomery Clift was another celebrity who lived several of his incarnations as the opposite gender from the one by which we knew him best. In fact, of his forty-five past lives, twenty-nine were spent as a female, which is a likely explanation for the bisexuality of his final lifetime. He's also a spirit who, while determined to grow and learn toward his soul's greatest perfection, never did quite become comfortable inhabiting a human body of either gender, and he's opted to accomplish the rest of his growth and learning on the Other Side.

His life in fifteenth-century Scotland was spent as a woman named Blair. If Blair was guilty of anything in that incarnation, it was of trying too hard, to the point of rigidity, and then being confused about why all that effort didn't result in happiness. Blair was an amazingly bright girl. She was the only child of very strict parents, both of whom happened to be scholars. They expected absolute obedience and academic excellence from her, and she complied without complaint or resentment. Extremely introverted and physically frail, she had no interest in trying to make friends or pursuing any relationships outside of her immediate family.

She left home when she was seventeen, sooner than she'd planned, through an arrangement brokered by her parents. A friend of her parents, of whom they were very fond, happened to be a wealthy land baron and had lost his wife suddenly. He needed a governess for his four young children. Blair was the perfect candidate and loved the idea of teaching and taking up residence in a safe, private, and already familiar environment. Fluent in six languages, skilled in math and the sciences, and especially enthralled by Greek mythology, Blair was determined to inspire her captive little students and to share her passion for learning. She demanded perfection from them, whether in their homework, in their behavior, or in their postures as they sat at their custom-made pine desks. She worked even harder than they did, planning their lessons, correcting their homework, and devising ways to help them in the areas in which they struggled. It was a source of enormous frustration for her that, unlike her at their age, they were more interested in playing or spending time with friends or in indulging in typical childhood silliness. They may not have always appreciated Blair's no-nonsense approach to education or her impatience with their slightest misbehavior, but in their heart of hearts they appreciated her utter commitment to their well-beings, her confidence in their abilities to excel, and even the sensitive, somewhat awkward shyness hiding in the shadows behind her intellect. They knew she loved them, and they took great delight in their occasional ability to make her laugh, a laugh that always seemed to startle her a little and inspire her to quickly look around, as if she were worried someone might catch her at it and scold her.

The children's father was enormously pleased with Blair's work and her presence in his household, and she deeply admired him. Despite their mutual fond respect, they stayed strictly within the boundaries of an employer–employee relationship. When his children were all grown and out of the house and Blair's governess services were no longer needed, he invited her to accompany him while he satisfied his lifelong dream to travel to Egypt and explore the pyramids. More out of loyalty to him and concern for his somewhat fragile health than out of any sense of adventure, Blair accepted his invitation. She planned afterward to return to her parents' home and care for them in their final years, but she didn't leave Egypt alive. She contracted a fatal intestinal virus, which, in her last incarnation on earth, cell memory reactivated in the form of Montgomery Clift's chronic dysentery.

In another incarnation, this one in Hungary in the mid-1600s, he returned as a boy named Janos who, with his twin sister Eva, was born to a pair of successful musicians. They lived a life of privilege and creativity, encouraged from their earliest childhood to find and pursue their greatest passions. For Eva, that passion was acting. For Janos, it was writing. Devoted to each other from the beginning, the twins dreamed of Janos writing brilliant plays for his sister to perform; she would achieve stardom and the two of them would become as celebrated as their parents. And they were both willing to work hard toward that dream. Eva studied with a Shakespearean acting teacher who lived nearby, and Janos was tutored by a playwright his parents had worked with in local theater productions.

Janos was nineteen when he finished writing the first play his tutor considered worthy of producing. Eva was trained and talented enough to admirably

tackle the lead female role. They both had large, fragile egos, which meant that they didn't take criticism
well, particularly from each other. They were both
perfectionists, so if Eva changed so much as a word of
dialogue—even if it seemed to make no difference to
anyone else and only felt more comfortable to her—
Janos would fly into a rage, while if he suggested an
alternative way of delivering a line, Eva was likely to
storm off to her dressing room. "One day," he would
frequently tell her in one of their flurries of artistic
differences, "I'll take up acting myself and show you
how it's done." This would invariably make Eva turn
away to stifle a smile, privately believing that he was
far too shy to ever be able to face an audience and survive the experience. They knew, perhaps too well,
how to push each other's buttons when they needed
outlets for their frustrations, but God help anyone else
who dared to criticize either of them in the other's
presence. Their parents were occasionally exasper-
ated but more often amused by how the twins' similar
temperaments formed an unbreakable bond between
them while also causing some of their most ferocious
battles.

Both separately and together, Janos and Eva achieved
their goals of being as artistically successful as their
parents, and they enjoyed a certain amount of celebrity

status throughout Hungary and central Europe. Neither of them ever married, although Eva enjoyed a long, rather scandalous affair with a Serbian despot and Janos maintained an ongoing homosexual relationship with a flamboyant actor named Hugo, who'd had a small role in one of Janos's plays. When Janos died of tuberculosis at the age of thirty-nine, Eva was inconsolable. She abandoned her career, saying that performing onstage was too constant and painful a reminder of her brother for her to continue. She went into seclusion in the home her parents left to her when they passed away, and she died there of congestive heart failure when she was seventy-one.

In their most recent incarnations, Janos and Eva were known as Montgomery Clift and his dearest, most loyal friend and cast-mate, Elizabeth Taylor.

BEA ARTHUR

When Bea Arthur completed her thirty-ninth and last incarnation in 2009, she was joyfully ready to leave this world behind and go Home to resume her busy, productive, eternal life on the Other Side. Her past lives seem to have had a recurring theme of discipline—how to live within it and how to administer it in ways that would inspire rather than discourage.

One lifetime took place in late eighteenth-century France. Her name was Cerise, and she was born to a professor and his socialite wife, both of whom were very concerned with status and image. It was a privileged but emotionally barren life. Cerise was given a lot of attention but very little love, as if the sole purpose for her existence was to present a perfect appearance at all times, because anything less might reflect badly on her parents. From an early age Cerise was taught etiquette, art history, music appreciation, equestrian skills, classical dance, floral arranging, fashion, and other socially oriented accomplishments. At the age of fifteen, she was sent to an exclusive Swiss finishing school, where her education in making an excellent impression continued. She was a superb student but also an intensely lonely one. She'd spent all her young life trying so hard to earn her parents' love and approval yet was always made to feel as if she could never quite live up to their expectations and therefore not worthy of their affection. By the time Cerise graduated from finishing school she'd become a harsh, angry young woman with a quick wit, which often expressed itself in the form of a harsh tongue.

Rather than return home to her emotionally unavailable parents, Cerise remained in Switzerland to work at the school and soon became its headmistress. Her students found her to be strict and inflexible, intolerant of their problems, but a knowledgeable, thorough, and well-prepared leader. She did finally find a source of unconditional love; through her equestrian training she'd come to adore the school's horses and spent every available moment caring for them, grooming them, training them, and talking to them. The stables had to be expanded as she began rescuing neglected and unwanted horses from the surrounding villages.

In time her highly valued position at the school, along with her carefully cultivated social graces, attracted the attention of one of the school's benefactors, an older wealthy widower who was in search of appropriate companionship. He courted Cerise for a year before marrying her. While they didn't love each other, Cerise agreed to the marriage based on her suitor's agreement to donate a substantial amount of money to the care of the school's horses, to which she was so devoted that she considered them hers and visited them almost daily.

Lonely as she was, Cerise was kept busy with running her husband's elegant household and expertly indulging his love of socializing and entertaining. She might have found herself content in her marriage, but in her late twenties—two years after her lavish wedding—she discovered she was pregnant. The thought of bringing a child into the same kind of loveless, shallow home in which she'd grown up was horrifying to her. At the school, and with the permission of the new headmistress, she hand-selected a group of girls and taught them everything about taking care of the horses—not just feeding them but also talking to them, spending time with them, and making them feel wanted, safe, secure, and adored. When she felt certain that her beloved horses were in good, reliable hands, she waited until her husband was asleep one night, selected a dueling pistol from his prized collection, and at five months pregnant, took her own life in the grand ballroom of their silent, lonely house.

It's worth mentioning that there is no standard punishment from God for those who commit suicide, even a suicide during pregnancy. Today, Cerise would have been diagnosed as severely clinically depressed, exacerbated by the inevitable hormonal impact of being pregnant. Suicides that happen as a result of mental illness are compassionately forgiven by God for exactly what they are: acts of desperation by those whose minds aren't clear enough or healthy enough to make rational decisions. So it makes perfect sense, in God's perfect creation, that Cerise and her unborn child were safely Home within seconds of the gunshot.

Bea was named Petra when she was born in Germany in the early 1800s, and her life was every bit as disciplined as Cerise's but with a much more positive purpose. Petra's parents, whose income was modest but comfortable, adored their daughter and were pleasantly shocked to discover when she was eight years old that she was a prodigy, with a voice perfectly suited to opera, which also happened to be her passion. With financial help from family members, Petra was sent to Munich to study at a small, prestigious school with a strict regimen and brilliant teachers. Petra thrived in the structured atmosphere and became a skilled and popular young operatic contralto. She was at her happiest in front of an audience. Her parents were enormously proud of her and never missed a performance.

Tragically, when Petra was only nineteen her beautiful voice began to weaken, until eventually she was unable to sing. By the time she was diagnosed with throat cancer, it was too late for treatment of any kind. She died the day before her twentieth birthday.

When she returned as Bea Arthur in 1922, she brought cell memories of an insistence on discipline, conflicted feelings about families and relationships, a love of performing, an equally deep love of animals, and, sadly, a vulnerability to cancer, which is what ended her final incarnation.

DICK CLARK

America's Oldest Teenager, television icon and legend Dick Clark, completed his forty-third and final incarnation on April 18, 2012. It's interesting that even though he was eighty-two when he went Home, the heart attack that ended this lifetime was only his fourth exit point; he'd scheduled his fifth to occur at the age of ninety-six but couldn't bear the thought of spending another thirteen years in a body that was becoming increasingly debilitated with no hope of significant improvement. He was ecstatic to find himself on the Other Side again, by the way, where a huge crowd of adoring friends and loved ones greeted him. Michael Jackson, Elvis Presley, and Buddy Holly were among the first to embrace him at the joyful reunion.

A remarkable twenty-two of Dick's past lives were heavily involved with music. Both on earth and at Home, his spirit naturally resonated with it and understood its power to inspire and unify. He lived a brief life in ancient Egypt, for example, as an accomplished harpist in the court of Djer; he was the musically gifted son of Johann Sebastian Bach, named Wilhelm, who, despite his talent, died in poverty; he was a sitar player who traveled with his itinerant family of musicians throughout Persia; and he composed sacred meditation music during his lifetime as a Tibetan monk.

While those incarnations most certainly had a cumulative effect on the man we knew as Dick Clark, the one that was undoubtedly his point of entry began on a slave ship in the early nineteenth century. His mother was among a large group of slaves being transported from west-central Africa to America. Her profound stress and fear, along with the deplorable conditions on the ship, contributed to her death during childbirth, but her newborn son managed to survive with minimal care until the ship arrived on the Virginia coast. He was promptly purchased by a wealthy older couple named Madison, partly out of pity and partly because they were sure a tiny infant with such a remarkable will to survive could be molded into a very valuable slave on their thriving tobacco plantation in the Roanoke Valley.

They named him Jeffrey, and they arranged a nursery for him in a small, rarely used wing of their mansion. They denied the servants access to that wing of the house without explanation and put their nineteen-year-old daughter Mary, who still lived at home while studying to be a schoolteacher, in charge of Jeffrey's care and feeding. It was understood from the very beginning that the Madisons didn't want anyone to know they were raising a black child within their own opulent walls. Jeffrey became the family secret, well-fed, nurtured, and taught by Mary, lonely and well aware that he wasn't to be seen or heard and that the vast majority of the magnificent house was off-limits to him. The Madisons' intention wasn't to imprison him, although that was the effect. Their intention was to produce a healthy, educated, loyal slave who understood the inner workings of the plantation and would someday become its general overseer, with none of the other slaves ever to know where he came from or that he was actually their boss's eyes and ears in the fields and in the slaves' quarters.

Mary, in particular, was very kind and attentive to Jeffrey, spending long hours playing with him, teaching him, reading him bedtime stories, and singing lullabies to him while he fell asleep, moved by the magically calming effect even the simplest music seemed to have on him. Her mother was a locally renowned pianist, holding weekly recitals on her grand piano in the family's drawing room. Even as a toddler Jeffrey would crawl into the closet of his nursery, where he could hear the music most clearly, and listen, mesmerized and deeply affected, joyful at recognizing the sense of peace it created in his soul but heartbroken that, for reasons he never quite understood, he was required to remain separate from it.

Jeffrey, Mary discovered, had a brilliant aptitude for math, finance, and business. Mr. Madison was delighted to find that he had his very own free accountant and advisor at his command, and by the age of thirteen Jeffrey had earned enough trust and developed enough knowledge of every aspect of the plantation to have blended in with the family's other slaves. He worked in the fields during the day and discreetly worked on the accounts with Mr. Madison at night. He still wasn't allowed into the main house or into the drawing room for Mrs. Madison's weekly piano recitals, but he would sit in the darkness beside the open window and cherish every note, every chord, and replay them over and over in his dreams.

One night, when Jeffrey was fifteen, a guest at one of the recitals spotted him "lurking" outside the drawing room window. Assuming he was one of the slaves trying to break into the house and, at the very least, rob the wealthy group gathered inside, he ambushed and killed him with a single shot to the heart. The Madisons hid the depth of their grief from the rest of the world, but they secretly honored Jeffrey by burying him in an unmarked grave in the family plot.

In his next incarnation, Jeffrey returned as Dick Clark, bringing with him that same brilliant business mind, his historic passion for music, and his equally passionate determination that no one should ever, for any reason—including the color of someone's skin—be denied access to its power.

ED SULLIVAN

A truly legendary entertainment writer, TV host, and star-maker, whose twenty-three-year CBS series, *The Ed Sullivan Show*, remains to this day the longest-running variety show in television history, Ed Sullivan ended his thirty-sixth and final incarnation in 1974. And considering his past incarnations, it's hard to imagine that he could have spent his last lifetime on earth doing anything else.

In sixteenth-century England, thanks to William Shakespeare and many others, theater was thriving. Ed, whose name was Pierce (either his first or his last name), was one of the most influential and most invisible, behind-the-scenes theatrical powers in London. Born to a life of wealth and privilege in a very well-connected family, Pierce had been mesmerized by the world of theater since he was a child. He'd aspired to be an actor, but a point came when even he had to admit that he had no acting talent whatsoever. He then tried becoming a playwright but found that it didn't hold his attention long enough for him to complete even a single play. Finally, when he least expected it, the answer presented itself in the form of an extraordinarily gifted young actor, who had not yet been discovered. Through family contacts, Pierce was able to arrange an audition for him, which triggered for him a long, prestigious acting career and set Pierce on the path he would follow for the rest of his life.

Pierce made it his business to connect worthy actors and playwrights with those who could put their talents to good, profitable use. And he charged those actors and playwrights a fee for the connections he could provide. He certainly didn't need the money, but it was his belief that people devalue and take for granted the things they get for free, and he wasn't about to be devalued or taken for granted. The word "agent" never entered his mind, but that's essentially what he became—a discreet, behind-the-scenes, smart, and very, very particular agent. He insisted that actors audition for him before he would agree to represent them, and he immediately dismissed those he considered less than exceptional. As far as he was concerned, if he wanted to use his influence to promote a mediocre actor, he could promote himself. Playwrights had to prove their worth as well. If Pierce read a playwright's work and was excited by it, he was an enthusiastic advocate. If he wasn't impressed, he dismissed that playwright without a second thought.

Pierce wasn't just smart and knowledgeable about theater. He was also a shrewd agent and a great listener, and would absolutely never tolerate unfairness against his clients. He attended every audition. If his client performed poorly or wasn't cast, Pierce had no objection. If a client wasn't cast because the client's family was involved in a long-running feud with the playwright's family, or because the director had already promised the role to his untalented brother, Pierce was outraged yet smart enough to devise a weapon to combat that outrage.

Between the conversations Pierce had with his clients and the information he picked up at parties with the theater crowd, he had an encyclopedic knowledge of secrets, which those in power would rather not have become public. For added insurance, Pierce kept meticulously detailed journals of those secrets, though he only used them in the strictest privacy and as a last resort, if a client was being treated unfairly. He might say to a philandering director, "I'm sure you would rather it not become public that on the sixteenth of June of this year . . ." or to an unscrupulous producer, "Wouldn't you prefer that your recent financial irregularities remain strictly between us?" It was an incredibly effective way of negotiating, and to those who accused him of extortion, he would simply reply, "If you'd treated my clients fairly and hadn't provided me with such explosive ammunition, we wouldn't be having this problem to begin with."

Pierce himself was a very discreet, unpromiscuous homosexual. He and his disabled sister, whom he adored, lived together in a beautiful country home and were inseparable throughout their lives. Pierce died in that lifetime of an aneurism at the age of fifty-one, having made a far greater contribution to the British theatrical world than anyone would ever know. (This incarnation was the beginning of Ed Sullivan's love of the entertainment business, his flair as a gossip columnist, and his treasured relationship with a woman who was once his sister but who accompanied him on his final incarnation as his wife, Sylvia.)

It was in the 1800s that he took his passion for great talent on the road, when he inherited his parents' traveling carnival. He toured with it throughout the American South, expanding it from a handful of rides, games, and "freak shows" to a platform for singers, dancers, jugglers, magicians, and others. His name was Harry, and he and his twin brother, Allen, who handled the carnival's finances, enjoyed a great deal of success due to, for the most part, Harry's uncanny instinct for the acts that his audiences would enjoy and his resolute determination to find those acts while also fulfilling his show's exhaustive commitments. Unlike his parents, who hired almost any performers who cared to show up, Harry was very particular and demanded that all potential employees audition before they became part of the troupe. He was also smart enough to be patient: if a performer impressed him, he kept him or her on the payroll, even if it took some time for that performer to become popular.

The only person from whom Harry would accept any argument contrary to his opinion was his wife, Joan, a former church organist he'd met at his parents' funeral. She shared Harry's instinct for talent, and no one became part of the troupe without her approval as well. If the two of them disagreed, or whenever Joan said an act either would or wouldn't catch on with their ever-changing audiences, Harry had learned over the years that Joan was invariably right.

One area where the two of them completely agreed, in defiance of a lot of public opinion in the South, was their insistence on hiring great talent regardless of that talent's race. Their traveling show proudly included several black performers. Because of that, there were towns in which their carnival was banned. That narrow-minded intolerance deeply offended Harry, but he quickly discovered that no amount of arguing or reasoning was going to change anyone's mind. So, at the first sign of any resistance, Harry chose to move on rather than subject his black employees to the insult of discrimination.

With those experiences firmly locked in his cell memory, it's no wonder that Ed Sullivan refused to cooperate with the network's hesitation at booking African American performers on *The Ed Sullivan Show*. Thanks to his insistence, the Supremes, the Jackson Five, the Temptations, the Four Tops, Sammy Davis Jr., and countless other superstars were given the national exposure and respect they richly deserved.

Harry continued a life he loved until it suddenly ended with a burst appendix when he was eighty-three. He began his incarnation as Ed Sullivan a remarkably brief four years later.

AUDREY HEPBURN

Superb, elegant, and unforgettable Academy Award–winning actress Audrey Hepburn completed her forty-third and final incarnation in 1993. While it was her iconic movie-star brilliance on-screen that will live on for generations to come, it was her remarkable soul that set her apart from the rest. Audrey Hepburn was a highly advanced spirit known as a Mission Life Entity.

Mission Life Entities essentially say to God, when they begin charting a new incarnation, "Wherever on this earth you need me, I'll willingly go." They'll sacrifice their comfort and their yearnings for Home in the name of the mission they've signed on for—not to convert or preach any specific religion or dogma but to compassionately rescue, reconnect, affirm, ignite, and celebrate the spirit of the divine in every child they encounter, whatever their belief systems.

They can be found in any and all walks of life, and they work the hard way up through the spirit ranks, writing exceptionally difficult life charts for themselves so that there's no level of life on earth that they can't relate to. A Mission Life Entity's path to achieving purpose is filled with hardship, turmoil, and disappointment, but in exchange is a feeling of profound satisfaction and a journey of the soul that only a rare few choose to take.

In a sixth-century incarnation, for example, Audrey was a male, a great East African hunter whose village was decimated by a drought. While most of the residents relocated in search of food and water, some of the elders were too old or ill to move and would have been left behind to die if he hadn't stayed behind to care for them as best he could. He sacrificed his own nourishment to feed them and lost his life to malnutrition in the process of saving their lives.

In eighth-century China she returned as a woman who sold herself into prostitution to feed her brothers and sisters when their parents were killed for their landholdings.

In ninth-century India she was a male again, a Hindu monk who devoted his life to gathering food and clothing to hand out to the children and elderly he found begging on the streets of Mumbai.

The first incarnation in which she was born into privilege took place in the eighteenth century in St. Petersburg, Russia. Her name was Karina, and her parents were very well connected, both socially and politically. Eager to raise a child who would be a credit to them, they decided when she was five years old to hire a number of tutors to discover and then guide whatever extraordinary talents their only child might have. Karina showed no ability or interest in art or music but, as happened in her incarnation as Audrey Hepburn, she had incredible potential as a ballerina. She began studying ballet at the age of six and fell in love with everything about it, from the discipline to the beauty to the feeling of being transported to a whole other plane of existence when she was performing, as if dance somehow set her soul free to express its joy.

By the time Karina was fourteen she'd become somewhat of a celebrity. She was delicate, petite, and exquisitely beautiful, with blue-green eyes that were rimmed by double rows of lashes. She attracted a number of suitors who knew it elevated their status to be seen with her in a seemingly endless whirl of social events.

Her future husband appeared when she was seventeen. His name was Vadim, and he was in his early forties, incredibly wealthy, and politically influential. Karina was a dream come true for him—a young, gorgeous, celebrated woman with important, well-connected parents who thought that he was a brilliant match for their daughter. For her part, Karina was fond of Vadim, appreciated the rapt interest he took in her and her career, and was very pleasantly surprised at his quick-witted sense of humor. With overwhelming encouragement from everyone around her, she agreed to marry him. They had a huge, magnificent wedding on her nineteenth birthday, and their marriage seemed to be an enviable success for its first several months.

Initially, Karina had thought very little about an invitation she'd accepted to be a guest performer and speaker at an orphanage in Moscow, a city where a new ballet school had recently been established. But after she'd arrived and begun to get to know the children and hear their stories, her heart broke. She'd lived such a sheltered life until then. Poverty, hunger, neglect, abuse, and abandonment—especially in the life of a child—were unfathomable to her. The longer she stayed in Moscow, the more passionately she felt that she wanted to spend the rest of her life here. She excitedly returned to St. Petersburg and announced to her husband that she was going to give up her career and teach ballet to orphaned and disadvantaged children. She may not have expected him to be thrilled, but she did expect him to respect her decision and appreciate its potential value.

As far as Vadim was concerned, he'd signed on to a marriage with a celebrated prima ballerina, not an orphanage dance teacher. He, her parents, her colleagues, and her friends all tried many times to convince Karina that she was making a huge mistake and to point out everything she was giving up, but all she could see was what she was gaining and how this opportunity was filling her heart in ways she'd never imagined. She understood when Vadim divorced her on the grounds of abandonment and when her parents began treating her like a distant relative, at best. A few close friends stood beside her and were proud of her, and they were instrumental in organizing fundraising benefits at which Karina performed with her students.

Her work eventually took her all over Russia and beyond—into what is now Poland and North Korea.

It was an exhausting, challenging, exhilarating, fulfilling life, though it was sometimes heartbreaking when the reality would hit Karina that there would always be more children in need of help and encouragement than she could possibly reach. As she passed to the Other Side at the age of eighty-one, one of many who fell prey to a flu epidemic, she was already planning another incarnation in which she would continue the work she had begun and use the spotlight of her celebrity to that work's advantage.

In keeping with that plan, and typical of a Mission Life Entity, internationally renowned star Audrey Hepburn became a goodwill ambassador for the United Nations Children's Fund (UNICEF) and traveled to the world's poorest countries, bringing food, clean water, medical supplies, and hope to children who, without her, might never have known what it was like to be embraced by someone who genuinely cared.

AVA GARDNER

Ava Gardner, who's lived eighteen lifetimes on earth and still has two more to go, spent an incarnation in fourteenth-century Japan that would set the stage for a challenge she would face time and time again in her pursuit of spiritual growth.

Ava, whose name in that life was Chiasa, was the daughter of a geisha and, at the age of ten, entered an okiya to be trained as a geisha herself. She excelled at dance, and by the time she was fifteen she had attracted the attention of a successful married jewel merchant named Nao, who became her patron and bought her way out of the okiya. He set her up in her own lavish house to secure her exclusivity. That he already had a wife was of no concern to Chiasa, since his was a fairly traditional Japanese marriage at the time. His wife was a quiet, subservient woman who was expected to simply tend to his house, be obedient, and not dishonor him in any way. Neither Nao nor his wife had married for love, nor had they pretended to, and they both found the arrangement to be perfectly satisfactory. Nao's pursuit of sex and other erotic excitement elsewhere wasn't just acceptable to his wife; it was to be expected.

Chiasa's parents had entered into that same kind of marriage—comfortable and to their mutual advantage but not a source of passion. Because geishas are not allowed to be married, Chiasa's mother had been forced to choose between her successful independence as a geisha and marriage to a man who promised security, wealth, and world travel. She chose marriage and had had a life most would envy, but she encouraged her daughter not to follow her path down the aisle. Instead, she taught Chiasa to pick and choose carefully from the many men who would be pursuing her, to wait until she found the patron who would provide well for her without expecting her to compromise her independence.

Chiasa followed her mother's advice as best she could and was very happy to have attracted such a desirable patron. What she hadn't expected, and had no idea how to handle, was the fact that she fell deeply in love with Nao. She'd been raised by her mother and by the okiya teachers to be much more detached than that and much more in control of her emotions, so she kept her feelings to herself. But she lived for their hours together and felt lost and only half alive when they were apart.

The arrangement between Chiasa and Nao was in its third year when Nao told her he was leaving for several months on a business trip to the Middle East. The truth was that he had simply found another geisha he preferred instead. Only two weeks after he'd supposedly left on his trip, an associate of his arrived at Chiasa's door with Nao's farewell note and his promise that, even though they would never be together again, he would honor his commitment to support her for the rest of her life.

Chiasa went insane with grief. It was bad enough that she believed that her life would no longer be worth living without Nao, but the unthinkable suggestion that he'd found someone better made her feel that the very best she had to give wasn't and never would be good enough.

No one ever saw her alive again. She withdrew into her beautifully appointed house and refused to eat, drink, and sleep until she finally, deliberately, wasted away at the age of nineteen.

An incarnation in Spain in the early 1800s was, in a way, a rebellion against her having allowed herself to be held emotionally captive during her brief life in Japan. Her name was Elena, and she was a great beauty. She was raised by a widowed father who adored her. When she showed a talent and interest in becoming a muralist, he hired a successful older artist to give his daughter private instruction. The artist's son, a prominent bullfighter named Roman, fell in love with Elena. She was also attracted to him, as well as his renowned machismo, and they married two months after they'd met.

The passionate aspect of their marriage vanished less than a year later, when Roman was gored by a bull and severely injured. His recuperation was long and slow. Elena tended to him in their home for a few weeks, but she'd bargained for an exciting life of prominence and celebrity, not the life of a housebound nurse with a husband who could no longer perform, either in the bullring or in bed. She began slipping away from home after he'd fallen asleep at night and spending an hour or two in the arms of an intensely handsome rancher named Franco whose bulls were greatly prized in bullfighting circles. Since both of them were married and intending to stay that way, they made every effort to be discreet, but Roman became suspicious and had Elena followed one night when she left for another tryst with Franco.

The next night, after Elena had fallen asleep, her wildly jealous, involuntarily impotent and incapacitated husband struggled into her room and stabbed her to death. She was thirty years old when she died.

When her incarnation as Ava Gardner began on Christmas Eve of 1922, she chose another lifetime as a great beauty with professional acclaim and the admiration of many men. She even chose another bullfighter husband (although not a reincarnation of Roman). What she began to work on, and will continue to perfect during her two remaining lifetimes on earth, was the elusive ability not to base her self-worth on her ability to attract others and to look inward rather than outward for the peace and fulfillment of her fearless, adventurous soul.

TED KENNEDY

The journey of Ted Kennedy's soul has a unique history. The lifetime by which we knew him best was his third and his last, and both of his previous incarnations took place in Rome.

He was a charismatic speaker and legislator named Chiron in the Roman senate in the days of Julius Caesar. He and Marc Antony were friends and mutually respectful colleagues, but Chiron had nothing to do with Caesar's assassination. Chiron was a pacifist and a brilliant debater who was passionately opposed to a governmental body that catered to the wealthy while ignoring the needs of the less advantaged, who were unable to help themselves. This compromised his popularity among the other senators. Two fellow senators, though, shared his sympathy for the poor and voiceless. They were often moved to outrage at the obvious inequities between the elite and the downtrodden, along with Chiron, and they would one day become John and Robert Kennedy, Ted's brothers. In Caesar's time, the three of them paid regular discreet visits to a former senator whose age and compromised health had forced him to resign his seat in the senate, a man to whom they turned for advice as well as an occasional scolding when their egos overrode their wisdom. He was a man they all met again in the twentieth century as their father, Joseph Kennedy.

Chiron's wife was a woman named Vita. Because their families were close friends, they'd known each other all their lives and were deeply committed to each other and to their only child, a son named Janus who'd been born blind and a quadriplegic. Janus died at the age of five, and Vita went Home four months later. The common belief was that she died of a broken heart, but the truth was that she took her own life because she found life on earth too empty and not worth living without her child.

Chiron was too grief-stricken to recover from the losses of his wife and son. He descended into what we would now call deep dementia and lived four more years in mute oblivion before dying of pneumonia at the age of forty-eight.

Ted returned to Rome as an archbishop named Gustavus in the 1500s. Like many members of the clergy in that era, he had a mistress, with whom he had two children. (His lifetime preceded the church edict that priests and bishops were not allowed to marry or father children. The edict had nothing to do with morality and everything to do with the church not wanting to bear the expense of supporting entire families in addition to supporting their clergymen.)

Gustavus was centuries ahead of his time in his very vocal belief in equality for women in the church. He traveled tirelessly, preaching the Gnostic faith throughout Italy and his mistress's homeland of Greece. He was widely known for his love of birds, and he built a sanctuary by a small stream near his home where he would successfully treat their broken wings and care for any abandoned nests of fledglings. He often confided to his mistress that while he believed in the basic goodness of humankind, he preferred the guileless, uncomplicated company of birds.

He was sixty-eight, and on a trip in Greece, when he was ambushed and sustained a blow to the head in a tragic case of mistaken identity. Gustavus died instantly. Cell memory recreated that wound in the form of a brain tumor centuries later, which ultimately ended the life of Senator Ted Kennedy on August 25, 2009.

It's worth mentioning that, even though they never acknowledged it out loud, Joseph, John, Ted, and Robert Kennedy were all well aware of their deep past-life connection. Joseph Jr., the oldest Kennedy brother, who was killed in action during World War II, had not shared previous incarnations with his father or siblings. As an interesting postscript to his story, he opted to take his second exit point in that World

War II battle rather than survive and proceed with his father's plan to elevate him to the U.S. presidency. He believed there was only one Kennedy who belonged in the White House, and he gladly left this earth for the Other Side to keep the path clear for a John Fitzgerald Kennedy presidency.

JACK LEMMON

One of the earliest of Jack Lemmon's thirty-eight incarnations was surprisingly barbaric for a man we came to know and admire as a gentle and gifted soul. His name was Chuluun, and he was the son of a prominent Mongol tribesman in Tibet. As the tribe leader's only male child, a great deal was expected of him, and he worked hard to live up to those expectations. From the time he was a very young boy, he was a fine horseman and an exceptional archer. By his early teens, he was riding side by side with the tribe's most fearless warriors, often capturing innocent able-bodied children and selling them into slavery throughout Tibet and Mongolia. It was assumed that when his father died, Chuluun would become the head of the tribe, until a "flaw" in his character was unearthed: the strong, brave, brilliant young tribesman found himself unable to kill any other human being, not even in battle.

Chuluun's father, mortified by his son's perceived cowardice, decided to challenge him by ordering him to publicly execute a slave who'd been declared disobedient. The night before the execution was scheduled to take place, Chuluun fled the tribe and vanished into the Tibetan mountains. His father's finest warriors eventually tracked him down, and by direct order of the head tribesman, he was brought home rather than killed as a traitor. By now Chuluun had met and fallen in love with a beautiful Nepalese woman named Odval. He begged his father to let him leave the tribe in peace and start a family with Odval so that his father would have the grandsons he'd always wanted.

Chuluun's father agreed on one condition: Chuluun was to join his fellow tribesmen in one last battle. If the battle were successful, Chuluun would be free to leave with his father's blessing. If not, he would commit his life to the tribe and follow his father's orders to the letter from then on, no matter how distasteful or unconscionable he might find them.

Chuluun, seeing this proposal as his only possible way of leaving in peace and starting a family with the woman he loved, agreed and set out for his last battle, determined to succeed and "retire" with his head held high. Tragically, he was killed—not by the enemy but by a young, overzealous tribesman who considered

Chuluun weak and wanted to make a name for himself within the tribe.

Chuluun's father deeply mourned the death of his son, and the young tribesman who killed him was executed for disloyalty to the wishes of the grieving tribal leader. Chuluun died in peace, knowing he'd essentially sacrificed his life for his refusal to kill and having no regrets about the price he paid for his beliefs.

Centuries later, in the late 1700s, Jack was born in Germany to a family of great wealth and privilege. He was extraordinarily bright, able to read and write by the age of three, and could accompany his mother—an opera singer—on both the piano and the violin by the age of five. Due to his insatiable interest in theology, his parents arranged for him to enter a monastery when he was nine years old so that he could concentrate on his studies without the distractions of traditional schools. He loved the peace, quiet, and regimented structure of the monastery and excelled in music, theology, and his other love, astronomy. His theological insights were so profound that he wrote many papers to the Vatican under the name Henry Heidle, some of which may still exist to this day.

He also had a gift for horticulture and started a successful vineyard on the monastery grounds. One of the great joys of his life was his widespread reputation as a mentor. Young men came to him from all over Europe for specialized studies in his many areas of expertise and found him to be a patient, loyal, and enthusiastic supporter, always the first to help them pursue their dreams. In fact, Henry's students started some of the most prolific family vineyards in France, and they rewarded their mentor with generous donations to the monastery.

He was in his late forties when he was elevated to the position of abbot. His informal mentoring program expanded into other areas, bringing music into the monastery as he taught violin, piano, and composition. He wrote hymns and formed a chorale to perform them, and the performances became so widely acclaimed that they attracted audiences throughout Germany.

At the age of seventy-nine Henry died of toxicity from a ruptured colon. He was buried in a modest grave overlooking his thriving vineyard, which was destroyed in 1860 when the monastery burned to the ground.

When Jack Lemmon was born in 1925, he brought a wealth of versatility with him from his widely varied past lives. His principles, his acting and musical talents, and his generosity toward those he mentored were alive and well in his cell memory in the incarnation by which we knew him best. The one negative cell memory from his lifetime in Germany was also the one that sent him Home this time around: he died of colon cancer in 2001. But he fulfilled all the purposes he'd intended in this and all his previous incarnations, so it's with the greatest peace and joy that he's decided he won't be spending another lifetime on earth but will be doing his mentoring work, as he puts it, "by remote" from now on.

JANIS JOPLIN

Iconic rock and blues singer Janis Joplin's most recent, troubled twenty-eighth lifetime ended in 1970 before she was thirty years old, but she'll be back once more, again as a profoundly influential singer, during the 2020 decade. As with so many of us, her struggles during this most recent incarnation took root hundreds of years ago, and they'll finally be resolved by 2085, when she'll go Home for the last time.

One of the lifetimes that profoundly affected her began in Portugal in the early 1500s. Her name was Valeria. She was the eleventh child of parents who were addicted to opium, and Valeria was born addicted as well. As they had done with their previous three children, her parents continued giving her opium rather than put her, and themselves, through the difficulty of withdrawal. And because what money they had was more likely to be spent on their addiction than on another mouth to feed, they arranged to sell her to a wealthy but completely corrupt Arabian couple, who renamed her Shada and claimed her as their own when they returned home to Medina with her. They kept her addicted as well, to maintain control over her, and then turned her out to prostitute for them when she was fourteen. She was given a minimum quota of money to bring home every day; in exchange, she was given food and drugs and continued residence in their lavish home. Since her survival depended on attracting as much attention as possible in the competitive prostitution trade, she dressed flamboyantly and developed a wild, seductive, self-assured persona on the streets, which was a sharp contrast to the introverted, unhappy addict she'd become by her late teens.

It was possibly inevitable that Shada became pregnant by one of her clients, but as far as her adoptive parents were concerned, it was the ultimate crime against the family. What man would want a prostitute with a pregnant body, after all? They kicked her out of the house and onto the streets, which were familiar enough to her that she was able to survive with the help of other working girls and a few sympathetic shopkeepers. While she had no experience with the concept of being a loving, responsible mother, she knew she didn't want her baby to be born addicted, as she was. So, from the moment that she discovered she was pregnant, she refused opium for the first time in her life. It was agonizing for her, and it was a miracle that the withdrawals didn't cause her to miscarry. But Shada gave birth to a tiny but otherwise healthy baby girl in an abandoned shed. She gently cleaned the baby, wrapped her in warm blankets that she'd stolen when she'd left home, and she left her baby on the doorstep of the Prophet's Mosque.

Knowing her daughter would be found and cared for, Shada then returned to the abandoned shed and overdosed on opium that she'd been stealing and saving for the occasion. She died on her twentieth birthday.

Janis continued to chart lives for herself in which addiction, if it were an issue, could be overcome, but cell memory kept winning out over and over and over again, including in her most recent incarnation, of course. The one chart she wrote for herself in which she believed her life would be simple enough, successful enough, and happy enough that she wouldn't give a single thought to substance abuse happened in Arkansas in the late 1800s.

Her name was Lloydene, a combination of the names of her father, Lloyd, owner of the local hardware store, and her mother, Irene, a homemaker. She was the baby of the family, with four older brothers who loved her and thoroughly enjoyed sharing their love of sports and all other typically boys' pastimes with their very willing little sister. Lloydene was a natural athlete and tomboy and could hold her own beautifully with her brothers, whether they were playing baseball, running races, climbing trees, or building a "secret" clubhouse within ten feet of the back door of their modest family home. When she wasn't playing with her brothers, she was helping her mother with chores, as a result of which she learned to cook, sew, and maintain a clean house. Her early years were happy, active ones.

School was much more of a challenge. She was dyslexic, which was undiagnosed in those days. It made her a slower reader than other students and the brunt of a great deal of teasing. She relied more and more on her extraordinary athletic ability to maintain any sense of self-esteem, and by the time she reached high school, two years behind schedule, she probably would have dropped out if she hadn't been given the opportunity to be the first girl in the school's history to compete at track-and-field events, at which she excelled. What should have resulted in acclaim actually seemed to invite still more cruel teasing, especially from her female classmates. They were jealous of all the time Lloydene spent with the boys and continued to delight in taunting her about her poor academic skills. The boys, in the meantime, had mixed feelings about competing against and often losing to a girl. She certainly wasn't feminine enough to attract their romantic attention. With her brothers now grown and out of the house, starting families of their own, it was a lonely time for Lloydene, a time when even her success as an athlete made her feel more isolated than included.

Romance did come along, once she'd left school. She met her father's new clerk at the hardware store, a young man ten years older than Lloydene who would have fallen in love with her even if she hadn't been the boss's daughter. They were married after a year-long courtship. Then they set up housekeeping near her parents' house and planned to have a large, happy family. Lloydene thought little of the fact that her new husband enjoyed a few drinks every night after work, and she occasionally joined him, but neither of them ever drank to excess, until their first child was stillborn and they were told that Lloydene would never be able to successfully bear another child. They began drinking more to ease their grief and the increasing loneliness of the house they'd intended to fill with children. Slowly but surely they became full-blown alcoholics, their drinking increasing with each new tragedy. Lloydene's parents died within a month of each other. The hardware store closed with the death of its owner, leaving Lloydene's husband unemployed. Their meager savings quickly disappeared. Her brothers helped financially as best they could, but they were struggling themselves too much to be able to help for long, especially since there was obviously no hope of repayment in the foreseeable future. Then one day, while repairing some loose shingles, Lloydene's husband fell from the roof of their house and broke both legs, incapacitating him and making it impossible for Lloydene to look for work as she'd planned, since there was no one else to take care of him.

When they were found side by side in their bed, both of his legs still in casts, no one was quite sure how long they'd been dead, but there was no question that they'd lost their lives to alcohol poisoning. Lloydene was thirty-two when a life had tragically ended that had looked so promising when she'd charted it. In many ways, the same could be said for her incarnation as Janis Joplin. What a joy to know that her upcoming lifetime, just a decade or so away, will be triumphant enough to reward her spirit for all of the pain it's been through and the courage it's shown in continuing to try again.

PETER FALK

Peter Falk's nineteenth life on earth ended on June 23, 2011, and he'll be back twice more before he feels he's accomplished all he hopes to in this world.

One of his earliest incarnations is a classic example of the concept of exit points. When we write our charts on the Other Side in preparation for an upcoming lifetime, we include five exit points, or five separate opportunities to return Home when we're satisfied that our purpose for that lifetime has been satisfied. The fact that we design five exit points into each incarnation doesn't mean we're obligated to wait around for the fifth one to arrive. Which exit point we choose is completely up to us, and as we compose our charts, we view our exit points with joy rather than dread. They signify a homecoming from this boot camp we chose to attend for our own reasons. And while from our point of view on earth there is nothing more heartbreaking than the death of a child, in the context of eternity, that death is simply a spirit who accomplished what it set out to do, chose to take its first exit point, and returned to its busy, blissful life on the Other Side.

Sometimes the purpose for a soul incarnating and then going Home again so soon isn't immediately apparent. But if you look at the situation on a much grander and more spiritual level, the purpose becomes clear.

Peter Falk was once born in twelfth-century Scotland. His name was Ian, and he was the sixth and last child of a merchant seaman and his wife. Ian's father was away from home for months at a time. His mother was, in a word, demented. She went on long, frequent drinking binges, leaving her children for days on end in a cold, damp, filthy house, alone and without food. Neither parent was home when Ian came down with pneumonia, exacerbated by malnutrition. When he began struggling to breathe, his oldest brother Colin ran a mile to their nearest neighbor for help. Ian didn't survive his illness, but when the neighbor—a wheelwright who lived modestly but comfortably—saw the deplorable conditions in which the children were living, he took them home with him. Ian's mother and father were too ashamed to find and reclaim their children, all of whom eventually found other homes where they were well cared for. Ian, then, by opting to take his first exit point, had made it possible for his five siblings to have the long, healthy, happy lives they would never have known without his life and death. And he joyfully returned to the Other Side, completely satisfied that he'd fulfilled a very worthwhile purpose during his brief stay on earth.

Peter's lifetime in England in the early 1500s displayed his same principled insistence on keeping his priorities in order, no matter what it took.

His name was Graham then, and he was a contented man, living in the English countryside near London. He had a devoted wife who was a great mother to their four bright, healthy children, and he had an occupation at which he was exceptionally gifted: he was a tailor, with a wealthy, well-connected clientele who thought him reliable and very creative. He loved his work and was proud to be able to provide well for his family.

He was shocked when he was summoned one day to an audience with King Henry VIII. The king, it seemed, had heard of Graham's extraordinary skills and wanted him to become the exclusive tailor of the court. It sounded like the opportunity of a lifetime, but there was a stipulation that made it impossible for Graham to accept: he would take up residence in the castle's servants' quarters, to be available twenty-four hours a day, and to avoid any distractions beyond his duties to the king and his court, he would have to leave his family behind. Of course, he would be able beyond his wildest dreams to provide for his family financially, but he would live hours away from them and see them rarely, if at all, for as long as his position remained secure.

Graham wasn't about to let anyone or anything, including the king of England, separate him from his family. He very respectfully declined the offer and returned home to resume his treasured peace and quiet. Within weeks, though, threats were made on his life and on the life of his oldest son if he didn't accept the king's offer. It was never clear whether the threats were initiated at the king's direct request or if they were the work of a small band of loyalists seeking the king's favor, but Graham had no intention of risking the lives of his family by staying to find out. He quickly packed them up and moved with them to the supposed safety of a small, out-of-the-way village in Ireland.

Unfortunately, the village wasn't safe enough. One night, as he left the shop that he'd bought to reestablish his tailoring business, he was shot in the right eye by a sniper, who was never apprehended. Gravely injured, he held on for almost a week, not wanting to leave his wife and children, before he finally let go and went Home at the age of forty-three. He never for a moment regretted his decision to choose his family over the status of working for the king.

It was no coincidence but actually cell memory in action that Peter Falk, at the age of three, had to have his right eye surgically removed because of a retinoblastoma, and no surprise that he excelled in sports, acting, and art with only half his vision. His past lives hardly paved the way to a lifetime of taking the easiest road to everything he accomplished, and accomplished so unforgettably.

WHITNEY HOUSTON

The beautiful, charismatic, magnificently gifted spirit we knew as Whitney Houston completed her nineteenth incarnation on February 11, 2012. She'll be back once more before she considers the earthly part of her soul's journey complete. She's charted that final lifetime to begin in Stockholm, Sweden, in 2019. She'll move to the United States at the age of twenty and eventually become as big a superstar in the world of medicine as she was in the world of music, developing an implant of some kind that will block the physical effects of substance abuse, significantly easing the recovery process and saving countless lives.

It's worth mentioning, by the way, that I've rarely seen a spirit with as clear a memory of her chart as Whitney Houston had. By the time she'd reached the age of forty-eight she'd already experienced three of her five exit points. When her fourth exit point came along, she knew that by choosing to go Home while she was still vital, in demand and "on top," she'd be sparing her loved ones, and herself, an old age that would have been marred by chronic, debilitating illness, the thought of which she found unbearable. Her death was not deliberate—most certainly not a suicide—but I'm sure that she'd charted it, and that she found a quiet, fearless joy in that awareness.

Without a doubt the most significant incarnation of Whitney's early lives took place in ancient Jerusalem. Her name was Ariel. She was tiny—no more than four feet ten when she reached adulthood. She was also headstrong and, from the time she was a child, always seemed to be a little lost, searching for something without quite knowing what it was or how to go about finding it. The family lived in a modest two-story limestone house, crowded among other houses on the noisy dirt roads of the Lower City. They were hardworking, private people who dutifully attended their nearby synagogue every week, where Ariel kept hoping some spark of faith would ignite her passion. Instead, she found herself, Sabbath after Sabbath, just going through the motions, empty and still searching.

Her mother, a sickly woman who sold homemade baked goods in the open-air markets, died of dysentery when Ariel was ten years old, leaving her in the care of a father to whom she'd always been especially devoted. Ariel's father, who'd always been a skilled stonemason, had discovered an artistic brilliance for creating mosaics, an art he happily taught his equally gifted daughter, when she wasn't busy with the cooking and household chores she'd learned from her mother and performed without complaint. After a few years of perfecting his craft, Ariel's father was summoned to a palace in the Upper City and commissioned to create a vast, elaborate mosaic for the wealthy residents' massive pool. His impeccable reputation quickly spread among Jerusalem's most powerful elite, and soon he was able to move his daughter and his studio to the Upper City and hire a crew to install the intricate mosaics he designed for the finest mansions and synagogues in Jerusalem.

Ariel was seventeen when her father lost his eyesight due to a tragic acid accident in his studio. It spoke volumes about her devotion to him that she not only cared for him twenty-four hours a day, tending lovingly to his every need, but she also completed the mosaics for which he'd been commissioned without anyone suspecting it was her work, not her father's, being delivered and admired. For two years she secretly filled her father's shoes, never sharing the news of his blindness and never leaving his side, except for hurried trips to the marketplace for supplies. It devastated him to be so dependent on her and, in his view, to be standing in the way of her pursuing a husband and children of her own. But their connection was so deep, and her appreciation for waking up every morning with a purpose was so fulfilling, that thoughts of a family of her own were never part of her dreams.

Those two years ended tragically, when Ariel's father, feeling useless and wanting to "set her free," took his own life with a carving tool while she was away from the house in search of his favorite wine. Her shock and utter devastation at finding him when she returned home sent her reeling into the streets, too numb to notice a highly emotional crowd into which she was enveloped and swept away.

Before she knew what was happening, she found herself near the foot of three crosses, where a small group of mourners had gathered to witness their loved ones' crucifixions. The grief she shared with the mourners compelled her to linger there, and she finally raised her head and found herself transfixed by one of the men nailed to a cross. Three women and a man were near him, sobbing and disconsolate, and for a brief instant, as she stood some distance away, his eyes met hers. Somewhere between that glance and hearing him utter the impossibly compassionate words, "Father, forgive them, for they know not what they do," Ariel became aware that the vague, unsettled search of her lifetime had come to an end, she'd found what she'd been looking for, and above all, her grief for the loss of her beloved father had somehow transformed into peaceful hope.

She later learned that the man on the cross was Jesus Christ, the Son of God, and she sought out and became a follower of the Apostle John, whom she'd seen with the three Marys at the crucifixion, during his time in Jerusalem. She ultimately set out on her own, quietly traveling to small villages and encampments to spread the teachings of Christ and devoting her life, her passion, and her inheritance to the hungry and the spiritually lost. When she died of exposure at the age of thirty-seven, she went Home joyfully, as she did in this most recent life, knowing beyond all doubt that Jesus was waiting to welcome her to the Other Side.

I will always wish I'd been blessed with the experience of hearing Whitney Houston sing as a child at the New Hope Baptist Church, a child whose soul once witnessed Christ's crucifixion and, through her extraordinary voice, shared that cell memory with the world for the rest of her lifetime. And to travel this most recent life with her, she brought her father from that incarnation in Jerusalem, in the form of her treasured cousin, Dionne Warwick.

ORSON WELLES

Brilliant writer, director, producer, and actor Orson Welles, in his thirty-one incarnations, has consistently developed his tendencies toward being a leader rather than a follower, an insistence on doing things his way or no way at all, a love of the spotlight, and a desire to indulge to excess. He'll be back for three more incarnations before he considers the earthly part of his soul's journey complete.

In approximately AD 1200 Orson Welles was a Samoan prince. His name was Manu, and he was the handsome, devout, and very obedient son of the island's ruler, an introverted man who appeared in public as infrequently as possible due to a facial disfigurement. As a result, the ruler didn't care for large organized celebrations. When Manu ascended to the throne on the day of his father's death, he took the completely opposite approach to ruling his people. He loved making public appearances; organizing and presiding over celebrations, parades, and religious ceremonies; and drawing crowds from all over the island, who were curious about their extroverted new leader. One of Manu's first accomplishments, and a tribute to his faith, was the construction of an elaborate shrine to the Samoan god Tagaloa, who had created the universe and was the father of all people and all other gods. Manu visited the shrine every day at sunset, kneeling to his creator and praying for wisdom, guidance, virility, and the obedient devotion of his people.

Manu, like his father, believed in polygamy and, through his team of messengers, spread the word throughout the island that he was ready to marry and would select his wives from all the young, virginal women who cared to appear before him for his consideration. They arrived by the hundreds, many accompanied by eager, hopeful parents offering gifts and promises as well as their daughters. After many months, Manu finally selected four wives for himself, based on their beauty, their intelligence, their manners, and their ability to pass a simple test: before escorting each woman into the small anteroom where she would wait to meet the king, his aide hid an exquisite pearl beneath a conch shell in the center of a table in that room. If the pearl was still there after the woman's long wait, she remained in contention. If it was gone, she was immediately excused as someone who could not be trusted.

Manu's wedding to his four brides was as lavish and massive as his other celebrations. All Samoan residents were required to attend and were rewarded for their efforts with feasts, parades, parties, and sunset prayers at the Tagaloa shrine. Manu's tendency toward excess was never more apparent, whether it involved food, his beloved fermented coconut liqueur, or the crowds he routinely orchestrated in a lifelong belief that big meant important. Plus, it was his official proclamation that at the celebrations his wives were to be afforded the same respect with which his subjects treated him. Any disrespect was to be reported directly to him, and the offender would be beheaded. In the end, thankfully, there were no beheadings.

Because he had chosen carefully, Manu's wives were universally respected and became popular for the respect they showed their subjects in return. Behind closed doors, Manu, to his wives' mutual and surprised relief, treated them just as respectfully—less like wives than like appreciated aides who enhanced his public image and kept him from being lonely. Manu's excessive appetites, it seemed, did not extend to sex, but he had a deep, innate dread of being alone.

Unbeknownst to Manu, a plot was brewing to overthrow him. A Samoan man named Omeri had brought one of his daughters to the king as a marriage candidate in a failed attempt to infiltrate Manu's inner circle and to then kill him. He was determined to take what he perceived to be his rightful place on the throne. He had no personal objection to Manu; he just felt that because his Samoan family lineage dated farther back than Manu's, he was far more entitled to rule. Fortunately, because Manu had inspired such loyalty among his subjects, word reached him about this plot, and rather than having Omeri beheaded, he had him and his family deported and permanently banished from the island.

Manu lived to the age of forty-five before dying of a variety of obesity-related illnesses. He and Omeri met again, many lifetimes later when they were known as Orson Welles and William Randolph Hearst.

Another particularly significant incarnation took place in the late sixteenth century. Francine rarely gives me full names of a subject's past lives, but in that lifetime Orson was known as Arthur Wainscott, a relatively minor Shakespearean actor who appeared in several productions at the Globe Theater before deciding that he could be every bit as successful a playwright as Shakespeare and could also gain considerable notoriety by writing and producing plays in which he would assume the starring role. He was indisputably a talented writer and actor, and he was certainly prolific, but he couldn't begin to compete with Shakespeare's success, a fact he blamed on Shakespeare's having gained favor with Queen Elizabeth I, to the exclusion of other equally deserving playwrights.

Arthur persevered, his own biggest fan and most impassioned believer. He continued writing, producing, and starring in his own plays at whatever venues he could find, convinced that he would be "discovered" sooner or later. While casting a production of a play he called *For a Farthing*, he met a fifteen-year-old aspiring actress named Beatrice. The instant she began to read for him, he decided he wanted to marry her. It was more lust than love at first sight, as well as an immediate belief that with her talent and his support he could make her as big a star as he still intended to be. Her ambition more than compensated for her lack of attraction for this man thirty years her senior, and they were married two months after that audition.

Arthur and Beatrice costarred in five of his productions, and while the productions were never failures, they continued to be only modestly successful. Beatrice hid her impatience as best she could, but privately she held an increasing disappointment with her husband and believed stardom was being withheld from her by his relative mediocrity. He was also so obsessed with his work that he would disappear for hours at a time to write yet another play he was sure would be the one that would finally secure his elevated prestige in Britain's theatrical community. It escaped his notice that his wife had begun disappearing from their flat for those same hours.

When Beatrice became pregnant, Arthur was surprisingly pleased. While he was a bit uncertain about how much time a child would inevitably take him and Beatrice away from their careers, he also found himself enchanted with the idea of an heir he'd never thought to have. To his and Beatrice's mutual surprise, the baby boy was born with a shocking head of red hair. (Both Arthur and Beatrice were raven-haired.) The only dramatically redheaded acquaintance Arthur could think of was a young man on the periphery of their circle of friends, an up-and-coming Shakespearean actor with whom Beatrice ultimately admitted having an affair. She had felt that the popular actor could put her career on a much faster track than Arthur could ever hope to achieve.

Arthur—devastated, betrayed, and humiliated in front of those in the theatrical community he had been so determined to impress—left Beatrice, the baby, and his career and retired to Scotland. He never wrote or acted again. He drank himself to death at the age of sixty-one, while Beatrice went on to a long, acclaimed career on the Shakespearean stage.

Though no one from that lifetime reappeared in the lifetime of Orson Welles, he did arrive in 1915 refusing to be denied the acclaim that he felt he'd been denied all those centuries ago.

JUDY GARLAND

Judy Garland's forty-one past lives have been filled with occasional joy and a lot of turbulence, which isn't unusual for souls as advanced as hers. That she plans to incarnate twice more, rather than "retire" to her blissfully busy life on the Other Side, speaks volumes about her determination to achieve the full potential of her extraordinary spirit. The Bible verse Luke 12:48 describes it perfectly: "To whom much has been given, much is expected."

Without question, her point of entry began in the early 1700s, near the newly founded city of St. Petersburg in Russia. Abandoned at just a few days old by her young, frightened, unmarried mother, she was sold to a childless Russian couple, not because they wanted a little girl to love and nurture but because they intended to raise a free laborer for their rudimentary dairy farm and believed that a girl child would be more pliable than a boy. As it turned out, they couldn't have been more wrong.

She was strong and smart, with hazel eyes that always had a hint of sadness in them, even when she smiled. They named her Darya, and they cared for her exactly as diligently as they cared for their livestock, having learned that proper nourishment led to more productivity and fewer fatalities. Almost as soon as she could walk, Darya was expected to learn the skills required to maintain a successful farm, everything from tending to the animals to baling hay to building fences to repairing roofs on the shelter structures. She never questioned these expectations or failed to live up to them; nor did she seem to notice that she was growing up with no friends and no education. What she did question was her lineage. Tall, slender, blond, and willowy, she bore no resemblance to her parents or to anyone in her extended family, all of whom were short and dark, and with thick, muscular bodies. Of far deeper curiosity, though, was the persistent feeling that she didn't belong with these people. There seemed to be an emotional disconnect between her and everyone around her.

She was eight years old when she finally asked her mother if this was really her family or if she possibly had another family somewhere that she was supposed to be with instead. Her mother lied, insisted that she was their biological child, and warned her never to ask such an ugly, disrespectful question again. Darya wasn't satisfied, but she kept any further questions to herself.

When she was thirteen, she was sent alone on the usual weekly trip to nearby St. Petersburg to deliver dairy products to a local market. As her horse and wagon headed back toward home through the narrow unpaved streets, they passed a small wooden church. Its modest congregation was just emerging from mass, and Darya was idly watching them when suddenly her heart almost stopped. Among the worshippers was a young woman who so eerily resembled Darya that Darya felt as if she were looking in a mirror. She abandoned the horse and wagon and ran to get a closer look. The young woman noticed her, and her hazel eyes widened in shock. In an instant, she looked away and hurried off, disappearing into a maze of alleyways.

Darya never returned home again. Instead, she haunted the small church, watching for the woman so identical to her, until finally one day the woman appeared again, to sing in the choir for Sunday mass, and she came face to face with Darya. Her name was Raisa, and while she couldn't deny their uncanny resemblance, she was too ashamed and too afraid to admit the obvious truth—that she was, in fact, the woman who had sold Darya to strangers all those years ago. She chose instead to befriend the girl and take her into her tiny, dank, one-room apartment, grateful for the companionship. Significantly, she also invited Darya to join her in the modest church choir, and Darya's voice, the voice that in her most recent lifetime made Judy Garland a legend, was heard and marveled at for the first time.

Needless to say, the relationship between Raisa and Darya was an emotionally complicated one. Darya believed with all her heart that, despite Raisa's denials and dismissive observation, she had found her birth mother, and a life by her side was where she belonged. She couldn't understand Raisa's refusal to acknowledge it and embrace her. Raisa, on the other hand, had kept the existence of her daughter a secret since the day she had given birth to her. She'd never made peace with selling her own flesh and blood, and she lived in fear that the couple who had raised Darya would seek retribution, if they learned that she'd betrayed the confidence they'd agreed upon the day Raisa had put her infant child into their arms. And so, as close as Raisa and Darya became, there was always a cautious distance between them, a withholding on both their parts that would never be resolved.

It was less than a year later when Raisa was stricken with pneumonia. Darya took tender, tireless care of her and was at her bedside when she passed away. Even in her last moments Raisa kept her secret, compounding Darya's heartbreak at losing her with so much love denied, each of them for their own reasons, and with so many questions unanswered.

Darya soon began drinking to dull her confused, shattering grief, and a week before her sixteenth birthday, she died of alcohol poisoning, without ever seeing her adoptive parents again or returning to the church where she had met the woman with whom she knew she belonged.

Judy Garland brought countless shadows and a world of unresolved pain from that life into her most recent legendary forty-seven-year incarnation—a childhood of hard work, that distinctive voice, a yearning for a family in which she felt she belonged, an ultimately fatal substance abuse, and finally, a complicated, unfinished, and utterly destined relationship with a woman she once knew as her mother Raisa but, this time around, knew as her daughter Liza.

MONTEL WILLIAMS

I hope you'll indulge this one departure from my focus on the past lives of celebrities we've loved and lost, but I couldn't resist asking my Spirit Guide, Francine, about my very-much-alive dearest friend for the last twenty-three years, Montel Williams. He's been through more than his share of difficulties in this life—prolonged illness, divorce, death that hit painfully close to his home and heart—without ever losing his positivism and his loving insistence on inspiring others. And in the vast majority of his fifty-four incarnations (exactly the same number as mine), including this one, he's charted a warrior theme for himself, having nothing to do with mindless aggression and everything to do with a fearless battle against perceived injustices.

Warriors are the fearless risk-takers of this world, the soldiers, pioneers, astronauts, firefighters, and countless other heroes in countless other professions who have the courage to step up to the front lines of a physical, moral, or spiritual challenge. If you've seen Montel in action as a motivational speaker, on charitable missions around the world, or in personal hand-to-hand combat against the multiple sclerosis with which he was diagnosed in 1999, you know exactly what I mean when I say he's as fine an example as we'll ever find of a warrior in action.

Of course, in this lifetime he started as a warrior with the armed forces, graduating from West Point and becoming a Navy SEAL. And in his life immediately preceding this one, at the end of the nineteenth century, he marched into battle as well, as a Greek army soldier named Basil in the Greco–Turkish War in which he lost his life. Deeply spiritual, as he's been in all his

incarnations, he was known among his fellow infantry-
men for leading them in a prayer for strength, courage, and divine guidance before they picked up their
weapons and armed themselves for whatever lay ahead
that day.

In the years before Basil stepped up to serve his
country and left for Crete, he was a family man, with a
wife and two children, who earned his living as a shipbuilder. He also happened to be engaged in a much
more personal battle. Basil's beloved younger brother,
Philip, had been deaf since birth. Their parents were
both gone by the time Basil was fourteen, and he happily took on the responsibility of caring for his brother
full-time. Philip was living with Basil and his wife
and children, more than earning his keep through his
love of cooking and carpentry, when he became the
target of a local government agency that insisted on
institutionalizing him. It was part of a movement at
the time to segregate those with physical challenges
from the rest of society, if for no other reason than to
keep them from procreating. Despite Basil's most passionate, most vocal efforts to the contrary, Philip was
taken away by the local authorities and confined in a
small sanitarium on the Aegean coast. Basil, devastated and outraged at the cruel unfairness of the decision, promised his brother that he'd be back to free

him, no matter what it took, as soon as he returned from war.

As he lay dying on the battlefield, Basil's last thought was that he'd broken his promise to his brother. When the two of them met again on the Other Side a few short years later, after Philip had fallen victim to a devastating plague of the flu sweeping through Greece, Basil didn't even get a chance to ask his brother's forgiveness. His brother was too busy thanking him for all the years of joy and loving care he'd given him. He wasn't about to hear an apology. They were inseparable at Home, enjoying every minute of being together and ultimately deciding to incarnate together again.

"It's my turn to take care of you this time," Philip told Basil. And, as agreed between the two of them, Philip returned as Herman Williams Jr., a firefighter for more than forty years, Baltimore's first African American Fire Department Chief, and Montel Williams's father.

I have to admit, as inspiring as I find all of Montel's lifetimes—including the one he's living now—I haven't stopped smiling about one in particular since the day Francine told me about it. It was the early 1800s, and his name was Cooper, which could have been either his first or his last name. He was a tall redheaded Irishman who owned a sugar plantation in South Carolina. He shared his antebellum mansion with his wife, their six children, and his elderly ailing mother, a retired school-teacher. They were a rowdy, happy Catholic family who attended mass every Sunday.

One day Cooper was returning home from a neighbor's farm when he found a young, frail black girl lying very still beside the road. She was alive but unconscious, having fainted from dehydration in the hot summer sun. He picked her up and rode quickly home with her, where she was revived and gradually brought back to health.

Her name was Jessie, they discovered. She was fourteen. Her mother was a slave on a plantation in Georgia and her father was the plantation owner, who was deeply embarrassed that she existed. Using the excuse that she was too small and weak to be of any use in the fields, the plantation owner had had one of his workers take Jessie away and drop her somewhere, anywhere, as far from the plantation as possible. Alone and frightened as she was, Jessie was glad to be away from that awful place and that awful life, where her mother seemed as resentful of her as her father was. Her mother had foolishly hoped that when she had gotten pregnant, the plantation owner would take good care of her and their child, but instead he had denied them both and sent her right back to work as soon as the unwanted baby had been born. Jessie would have died on that road if

Cooper hadn't rescued her, and at that point she hadn't been sure she cared anymore.

From that day on, Jessie was embraced as a part of the family. She really was a hard worker, tirelessly helping with the cooking and cleaning and child care in order to earn her room and board. She and Cooper's mother became great friends. Cooper's mother taught Jessie to read and write, and Jessie hand-fed her every meal, bathed her, cleaned her soiled linens, and treated her with heartfelt compassion, love, and respect. Jessie was also incredibly gifted with the many animals on the plantation. They gravitated toward her as magically as she gravitated toward them. One of the countless things Jessie admired about Cooper was that he was morally opposed to hunting, and it was strictly forbidden on his property. The family shared their faith with her, introducing her to God and Jesus and the Bible, and included her when they took turns saying grace while seated together at the dinner table.

When Jessie turned twenty, Cooper told her that if she wanted to set out on her own, to fall in love and start a family, he would not only understand, he would give her money to carry her for as long as she needed. She turned him down, unable to imagine a happier, more secure, more fulfilling life than she had right where she was. And that's exactly where she stayed for the next fifty years, without a moment of regret, repaying that kind man many times over for saving her life and then giving her a life.

Not until Francine told me that story did I understand why it was that the first time I met Montel, it felt less like an introduction than a reunion. I, of course, was Jessie, and I'm so blessed that he and I have chosen to go through our last incarnations together . . . again.

PART THREE

Discovering Your Own Past Lives

I wish for every one of you that you could travel back in time and explore the magic and miracles to be found in your own past lives. While ideally you could find a reputable regressive hypnotist to guide you on that journey, I know they're not always affordable or easy to contact, not to mention the fact that there are some shameless frauds out there who will tell you, probably for vast amounts of money, that once upon a time you were Cleopatra, or the Virgin Mary, or Napoleon Bonaparte. I shudder to think how many reincarnated Virgin Marys are walking around today not knowing they've been scammed. For the record, in my more than five decades of countless regressive hypnosis clients, I've come across exactly one celebrity—a British economist I've never heard of who lived in the mid-1800s. If you can locate and afford a regressive hypnotist, please don't go rushing in to see them with cash or credit card in hand until you've checked them out thoroughly, either online, from trustworthy referrals, or through the Better Business Bureau. Otherwise, please save your money.

There's a beautiful risk-free exercise you can try at home that won't cost you a single dime, and I'm confident that you'll find it both relaxing and fascinating. I hesitate to call it a meditation, because I've heard too many clients claim that they don't know how to meditate and don't have the time or interest to start learning. All you have to do for the exercise I'm about to give you is to sit or lie down in a quiet place where you won't be interrupted and simply visualize what I'll describe as we go along. Make a tape of yourself, or of a friend whose voice you find soothing, reading these pages and use it to guide you. Then just settle in, clear your mind, take several deep, cleansing breaths, and enjoy the trip as often as you want. It's risk-free, and it just might change your life.

First, Relax

Sit or lie down on something comfortable in a place where you feel completely at ease. Loosen any clothing you might be wearing that could restrict your breathing or circulation or distract you in any way. If you wear glasses or contact lenses, feel free to remove them. Your spirit's eyes are all you'll need for this sacred, magnificent journey.

Let your open hands rest gently on your legs with the palms facing upward and ready to receive God's energy and healing.

If you're lying down, keep your legs uncrossed to allow your life-giving blood to flow freely through them unimpeded.

If you're sitting, keep your legs uncrossed, and let the soles of your feet touch the floor.

Slowly close your eyes, silently shutting out every distraction, every source of stress and irritation around you, everything but the quiet assurance of these words.

Let the pure white light of the Holy Spirit form above your head while you take three long, deep breaths—in, then out, in, then out, in, then out. With each new intake of air, let the sacred white light above you draw closer, until, on the third breath, you actually feel its smooth silken comfort settle over you in its silent grace, like an impossibly soft, weightless cloak.

Your breathing should stay deep and rhythmic as your mind quietly focuses on your feet. Sense the soles, the arches, each toe, each bone and muscle, and with each breath you take, let the tightness ease, bone by bone, muscle by muscle, cell by cell, as if a divine hand is massaging you, soothing you, dissolving pain, resolving tension, opening each vein wide, and making each open vein receptive to the vibrant circulation coursing through it, bringing renewal, like water to a parched, neglected land.

That deep, life-giving warmth, that glorious vitality works its way slowly up your ankles, your calves, your knees, the muscles of your thighs, and into your pelvis and every cell, every vessel of your stomach. Your spine straightens, letting go of the anxiety it carries, like a heavy, invisible burden, as your lungs fill with clear, sweet air. Your heart pumps, as strong and joyful as the heart of a child, and the heat of rejuvenated circulation floods your shoulders, your arms, every finger of your hands with the relaxation they've yearned for without even knowing how much of your stress they've been holding so tightly and so vigilantly.

Your neck and your jaw luxuriate in the healing heat of freely flowing blood. Each muscle unwinds, releasing its own burdens, and your mouth slackens with relief. The furrows of worry in your brow vanish as that hand reaches again to absorb the tightness, then covers your closed eyes with tender healing. If grateful tears flow, simply smile and whisper a thank you to your Father for this blessed release.

While His hand covers your eyes, let the deepened darkness form a starless, black velvet sky in the center of which, as you watch closely, a tiny pinhole of gold light appears. It fascinates you, and you neither can nor want to look away from it, sensing something alive in it, something divinely familiar, a sacred glimpse of knowledge and your own eternity that you're almost afraid to believe but that you know, with growing certainty, is the impossible, miraculous truth.

The tiny gold speck of light comes alive, pulsating, growing. Your heart beats stronger. Your breath keeps time with the pulse of that glow in the black sky you've created. And with every breath you take, you release every pain, every hurt, every injury you've ever felt, physical and emotional, and you know beyond all doubt that you've finally learned all the lessons that cruel, nagging pain had to offer. You can now unclench your hands and soul and let it go. It's not a part of you, and it's of no further use to you. As that certainty settles in, you feel it begin to lift from your cells, your body, your mind, and your spirit, like the dark, impotent shadow it is, no longer able to separate you from your power, your effectiveness, and your connection to the divine lineage that led you to this extraordinary moment, in search of all the answers your spirit has held safe for you to find.

As every trace of your pain ebbs out of you, the golden light continues to grow larger and larger above you, its rays alive and dancing in joyful homage to the Creator you share.

Suddenly, without a sound, the huge pulsating light explodes in sacred fireworks of gold. Its glittering shower of stars descends toward you in a soft, healing powder that falls into your face, your hair, your shoulders, your arms, your feet, every pore of your skin, leaving you to glisten with vitality, your body reborn, your spirit purified and more energized than ever for the challenges that again drew you to earth from Home; stronger, braver, and newly inspired, ready to travel into its timeless past in the safe, unconditional love of your Father's guiding hand.

Now, Back Through This Lifetime

Your skin is still sparkling from that blessed shower of stars. Your relaxed, healthy body feels peaceful, powerful. Your mind has never known less worry or more clarity. You imagine yourself standing now, facing a thick green forest as the sky pales from midnight blue to the pastels of dawn.

Keeping your eyes closed, you move them slightly upward, as if you can look through your eyelids and focus on the bridge of your nose, just for a slow count of five, sending you even deeper into the treasures of your spirit mind, its memories, its wisdom perfectly intact, waiting for you to find your way to them.

Your eyes relax again, refocusing on that thick forest in front of you, and you're intrigued to discover a narrow, endless path that has opened among the trees. The smell of pine sweetens the air. Shafts of gold from the rising sun glisten through the branches to light the path. A curious realization washes over you, that this path is somehow familiar, and you take a tentative step toward it, asking your Father for the courage to proceed without fear toward whatever lessons you might find along the way. The white light of the Holy Spirit glows brighter around you, protecting you and reminding you that you're not alone, not ever, ever alone.

You find yourself moving forward into the sacred privacy of the pine-scented forest. You hear nothing but the occasional song of a distant bird and the rush of an unseen stream. You've never felt, never been so safe as you proceed along the path and find yourself in a sunlit clearing where, impossibly, a scene from your twentieth year in this life is in progress. You watch, mesmerized by its intricate detail and its clarity. Then, suddenly, you recognize that you're twenty years old again and you step into the scene you've come across.

You belong there. It's yours to celebrate and experience, not as a memory but as a real moment very much in the present tense.

If no scene appears right away in that clearing, just wait. Relax. You're doing nothing wrong. Be patient. Once upon a time you were twenty years old, so simply ask yourself what was going on in your life at that age. Was there a special Christmas that year, a first day at a new job, a last day of school, a birthday party, an apartment you lived in, a car you remember driving? Did you have a favorite movie, or song, or sport, or hobby, or television show that the scene in the clearing can blossom into? Again, relax. It will come.

And when it does, look around and notice every tiny detail—every smell, every sound, every face, every color, and most of all, every feeling you have about it. If you feel happy while exploring this scene, or especially healthy and young and vibrant, luxuriate in this opportunity to relive it and be infused with it until it reaches every cell of your body.

If the scene upsets you, or if at the age of twenty you were having health problems, either physical or mental, that are playing out in front of you, just observe the scene and remain separate from it, a safe distance away.

As you stand there, recognizing your powerful ability to travel back in time, offer this prayer to the one who gave you that ability:

May all the vitality, peace, and security my cells remember from my twentieth year stay with me and renew my body and spirit, today and always. But any negativity, conscious or unconscious, that I've carried with me as a burden from that same age, let it be resolved into the white light of the Holy Spirit that surrounds me, today, tomorrow, and throughout my happy, healthy, productive, innovative, spiritual life. Amen.

You return to the forest path, walking on with a stronger, rejuvenated step from your visit to the twentieth year of this life. Sun-speckled leaves brush gently against your bare arms in a soft breeze, massaging them with their God-given energy. You stop for a moment to listen to the singing birds, the soft rush of the nearby stream. You look up, beyond the towering branches, to a blue sky, where soft white clouds are moving slowly, silently by. You know you're safe and at peace and so blessed, and there is nowhere you would rather be.

Another clearing appears, and you move eagerly toward it, aware that it's there for you and you alone.

A scene from your tenth year in this lifetime, perfectly preserved, has been waiting for you to arrive. The instant you see it, you're ten years old again, leaving the path to join a different birthday, a different Christmas, a best friend, a first day of school, a favorite pet, a music lesson, a playground game with classmates, some event, no matter how trivial, as real as the day it happened.

Again, if nothing comes, relax. Be patient. Stay out of your own way and let your conscious mind help clarify the scene. What did your school look like when you were ten? Where did you live? What grade were you in? Who was your teacher? What was your favorite subject, or your favorite game at recess? What was your favorite food or your favorite place to eat? Even the smallest detail can make the scene in the clearing come alive, so just keep remembering until that happens. There's no hurry, no hurry at all.

When that scene appears, explore it. Notice everything about it. The happiness you find there is yours to keep, and any pain you find is only there to remind you that you were strong enough to survive it and move on.

You thank God for all of it, the happiness you cherish and the pain you learned from, and then you repeat your prayer:

*All the vitality, peace, and security my cells re-
member from my tenth year, let them stay with me
and renew my body and spirit, today and always.
But any negativity, conscious or unconscious, that
I've carried as a burden from the age of ten, let it be
resolved into the white light of the Holy Spirit that
surrounds me today, tomorrow, and throughout my
happy, healthy, productive, innovative, spiritual
life. Amen.*

Linger there for as long as you like, then return to
the path and move on, God's hand holding yours to keep
you from falling as your step quickens. You are eager
to see who and what waits for you in the next clearing.
Your conscious mind would have dismissed this journey as impossible, but your spirit mind is completely in
charge now, yearning to show you all it knows and the
lifetimes it's lived.

Then you come upon that clearing and stand in awe
as you realize you're witnessing the moment of your
conception, that miraculous moment when your spirit
entered the fetus that would be your body in this life.
Just as it remembers everything else that's ever happened to it, your spirit can remember its brave, blessed
trip from its Home on the Other Side. Don't waste this
treasure by letting your conscious mind interfere and

try to tell you it's impossible. Simply accept it, cherish it, and believe. Be grateful for the imagery that's playing out before your eyes.

Then, suddenly, you feel as if a hand is gently urging you away from this scene and toward the next clearing. You can sense it just beyond the last few trees. You step back onto the path and find yourself almost running to get to that clearing, unable to imagine what you'll find there but unable to wait another moment to see it.

There's nothing but darkness there at first. You step farther into the clearing, curious and unafraid. You feel a breeze nudging you along until the path and the trees behind you have disappeared, and you find that you're completely surrounded by the deepest, safest, most peaceful darkness you've ever experienced.

Gradually you become aware that your feet are no longer touching the ground. You're floating in the dark weightless silence, treasuring the sensation, so secure, so blessed, so perfect, so loved, until finally, impossibly, but somehow of no surprise to you at all, you're able to make out your own tiny hands in the darkness, your own tiny limbs, your own tiny feet, moving like shadows, but there's no doubt that they're real.

You know where you are. You know you asked to be here. You know you're just on a brief trip away from

Home and that very soon you'll be thrust into this rough, hard world called earth again.

In your very last moment before you left the Other Side for another incarnation, you felt the touch of God's hand, like a loving, reassuring kiss on your forehead.

Still floating through the darkness in your tiny body, Home-sick already but braced for this new adventure you chose and charted toward the further perfection of your soul, you pray again:

All the vitality, peace, and security my cells remember from the Other Side, let them stay with me and renew my body and spirit today, through my birth and forever. But any negativity I'm carrying with me from my past lives, let it be resolved into the white light of the Holy Spirit that is my divine companion in this warm, safe womb, today, tomorrow, and throughout my happy, healthy, productive, innovative, spiritual life. Amen.

And Now, The Journey Into Your Past Lives

Still floating in serene darkness, at peace and unafraid, you become aware of a brilliant purple light behind you. You turn and look directly into it, and it becomes so bright, so strong, and so all-encompassing that it's all you can see and all you want to see. You somehow know that it embodies perfect love, wisdom, and compassion, and you joyfully step toward it and into it, immediately able to sense God's tangible presence all around you.

A tunnel opens deep inside the purple light. You can see its gleaming golden walls, etched, intricate, and divinely compelling, and you eagerly cross its threshold.

Instantly you realize you're moving, gliding with thrilling ease through this gorgeous tunnel, and a miraculous certainty overwhelms you, the certainty that you're actually moving back in time, past that moment of conception you experienced, past other events and lives that your spirit has already resolved; and a voice inside you guides you with a whisper, "Go to the core of your most pressing cell-memory pain, that core called your point of entry."

You understand perfectly and know exactly where your journey needs to take you.

The same brilliant light that sent you on your way at the beginning of the tunnel greets you at its end, illuminating a vast map of earth. And now the voice whispers, "Wherever my first point of entry occurred, through the grace of my cell memory and my spirit mind, toward their desire to be healed, may my hand find that place on this map."

Neither thinking about it nor looking at the map, your hand raises to it and, moved by your spirit, very deliberately touches a specific location. You look to see where your finger has made contact and, with sublime faith, you simply say, "I willingly ask my spirit to take me to this significant place it remembers and show me the life and time I spent there."

Your spirit mind instantly obliges, and you're there, in a whole other life that was once yours, as real as the life you've temporarily left behind somewhere in a quiet room.

You look around to get your bearings. Your conscious mind will be attentive but not intrusive. You ask questions and answer them immediately, without thinking, without judging, without editing. There are no wrong answers. The words that enter your mind are the only words that count.

Where are you?

Do you know your first or last name? If not, it doesn't matter.

How old are you?

Are you male or female?

What do you look like? Are you tall? Short? Slender? Stocky? What color is your skin? What color is your hair, your eyes? What clothing are you wearing, if any? If you have trouble getting a clear image of yourself, find your way to something that will let you see your reflection—a mirror or a glass storefront, or a calm pond or stream, or a piece of metal—and simply describe in detail what you see.

What year is this?

Where do you live?

Do you live alone? If not, who lives with you?

Is there anyone around you whom you know in your life in the twenty-first century? Who were these people to you then, and who are they to you now?

Are you healthy or unhealthy?

If you're unhealthy, what is your illness or injury? When did it begin, and what caused it?

Is this a happy life or an unhappy one?

If it's happy, what makes it happy?

If it's unhappy, what makes it unhappy?

What is your life theme for this lifetime? Your spirit will understand and know the answer.

What is the best part of this life?

What is the worst?

You chose this moment you're visiting from your timeless history to reveal the point of entry, or the core, of your most difficult cell memory. What is it about this moment, this circumstance, or this life that so profoundly impacted you for every other lifetime to come? What led to it, and what is essential for you to understand about it?

Again, no editing, no judging, no hesitating. Talk. That's all. Say anything and everything that occurs to you. Your spirit mind has been waiting so long for this opportunity to unburden itself so that it can send healing messages to the cells of your body.

Whenever you're ready, and not a moment before, you slowly ease forward in this past life you're revisiting. Where were you a year later? Five years, ten years later? As that lifetime continued, did you satisfy the purpose for which you chose it?

Now, go to the moments before your death in that life, fearless in your absolute knowledge that your current life, years or decades or even centuries later, is all the proof you need that you never have and never will really die at all.

If for some reason, though, you find that watching yourself die in this past life is traumatic or upsetting, just be an observer, maintaining a distance from it and remembering that it's not happening now; it's an event you've already survived and you don't have to be afraid of it again. Focus on these new questions instead:

What illness or injury is causing this death?

Where are you?

Who, if anyone, is around you?

Are you reluctant or glad to be leaving this lifetime?

In the last moments of this incarnation, are you conscious of the sacred truth that you're about to return Home?

And just as the tunnel begins to appear to take you to the Other Side, freeze that moment, making everything stand perfectly still, and offer this prayer:

Dear God, I thank you for the courage to face that moment in this past life when my spirit mind and the cells of this body took on a burden I've struggled with ever since. At this moment of my death in that life, please let that burden and all other negativity I've been carrying be resolved in the divine white light of the Holy Spirit, then, now, and always, so that I can devote my joyful, eternal, unburdened freedom to thy service for the rest of the happy, healthy, productive, innovative, spiritual life with which you blessed me an eternity ago. Amen.

Finally, when you're ready for your visit to that life to end, I want you to travel back into this current body and this current lifetime on the slow count of three, relaxed and at your peak of health, faith, and peace.

You are no longer burdened by a weight you never consciously knew existed, so your spirit mind can cleanse your cells of darkness and soar with God's love for the rest of the eternity He promised you.

One . . . Your eyes slowly open . . .

Two . . . Refreshed and radiant with vitality, you lift your head . . .

Three . . . Fully awake and renewed, proceed from this moment forward, thanking yourself and your Creator for the new beginning you've given yourself by opening your mind and heart to the healing secrets you simply needed to find and resolve.

Amen.

Acknowledgments

A brief, very special thank you not only to the celebrities in this book, who in such diverse ways left indelible footprints on this earth, but also to everyone we have loved and lost, who is waiting for us right this minute on the Other Side.

THE NEW LUXURY IN READING

We hope you enjoyed reading
our new, comfortable print size and found it
an experience you would like to repeat.

Well – you're in luck!

HarperLuxe offers the finest in fiction and
nonfiction books in this same larger print size and
paperback format. Light and easy to read, HarperLuxe
paperbacks are for book lovers who want to see
what they are reading without the strain.

For a full listing of titles and
new releases to come, please visit our website:

www.HarperLuxe.com

2/13